Praise for *Legacy of Wisdom*

"Gabrielle Taylor has produced a unique and fascinating perspective on the subject of wisdom and living wisely that readers of all ages will benefit from. Just as importantly, it is as entertaining as it is illuminating."
—Steve Shiver, Amazon Book Reviewer

"A great book! Taylor has accomplished an impressive feat: documenting a treasure trove of family wisdom passed down through the generations, while also providing practical tools to help anyone more effectively navigate life's twists and turns."
—G. Riley Mills, cofounder of Pinnacle Performance Company and author of *The Pin Drop Principle*

"As someone who is fascinated by human behavior, how people make decisions and influence each other, wisdom has long been topic of great interest. In *The Legacy of Wisdom*, Gabrielle Taylor succeeds in the difficult task of offering the reader an original account of how wisdom plays a key role in our everyday professional and personal lives."
—Olivier Oullier, PhD. Strategist and professor of behavioral and brain sciences at Aix-Marseille University

Legacy of Wisdom

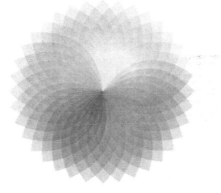

Gabrielle V. Taylor

Legacy of Wisdom
by Gabrielle V. Taylor

© Copyright 2015 Gabrielle V. Taylor

All rights reserved.

Published by: Taylor Strategy Partners, LLC

Cover and Interior Design: Nick Zelinger, NZ Graphics
Editor: Mark Graham Communications

Library of Congress Cataloging in Publication Data
ISBN: 978-0-9862074-6-4 (print)
ISBN: 978-0-9862074-8-8 (eBook)

First Edition

Printed in the USA

This book is dedicated to my daughters,
Brooke and Morgan, and in memory of my engaging
and formidable Grandma Valentine.

Table of Contents

Acknowledgments

On Christmas morning in 2012, I unwrapped what is the best Christmas gift I have ever received. It was from my husband, Dylan, and it was the gift of professional services from a firm that would assist in the development and completion of this book, which I had begun as a novice author a year earlier. Out of all the beautiful gifts, cards, and sentiments that have been given to me over the years, this one brought tears to my eyes because I realized the support he was giving to allow me to chase down an idea and a dream to give a special gift to my daughters and help celebrate my Grandma Valentine who had given shape to the meaning of wisdom and its uses. I owe my deep appreciation and thanks to my husband who, without fail, has supported me every step of the way. His unconditional love and devotion every day have been an inspiration and, without it, this book might not ever have been completed.

I would also like to thank Cara Lopez Lee, Mark Graham and Mark's group of experts at Mark Graham Communications for their tireless efforts to help develop, organize, and give rise to my book.

My special thanks to Brooke and Morgan, my precious daughters, who have been avid cheerleaders the entire way. Without their love, support and understanding, this book would not have been completed in this century. They were deeply generous as I shared our family stories of growing and learning moments that will ultimately foster a life built on wisdom. I know they allowed some of their personal stories to be told because of a deep commitment to their Mom's dream for this book.

I would like to acknowledge Colin Graham at Graham Publishing Group and his staff for their support and guidance. Many thanks to Nick Zelinger at NZ Graphics, who is the design guru extraordinaire behind this book.

To my family, most importantly my mom, Joyce Valentine, and my dad, Ben Regan, who helped recount and verify those details sometimes lost through time, thank you for your time and for everything. The love of a parent is tremendous. Both of my parents trusted, without question, that my goals and desires for this book would be a hopeful celebration of all that is intriguing and great in life and I want to thank them for their belief in me.

To my friends in Chicago, Pamela Locke-Mepham, Michael Pavia, Saretta Joyner, Valerie Tokars and Michelle Smith, and my friends in Denver: Nancy Mitchell, Michelle Brunschwig, Stacey Smith, Chantil Arciniaga, Erica Gillett, Kelly Dreyer, Dino Maniatis, Tommy and Jill Spaulding, all of whom listened patiently and offered enthusiastic support and advice on my writing endeavors, I thank you for being wonderfully unique and amazing.

In addition, I would like to thank Jayme Mansfield, Greg McKeown, Tan Le, and Geoff Mackellar, who generously gave me their professional guidance, support, and time. Their insights and thoughts were critical to my efforts. And, I would like to thank all of those around me who knew of my efforts with this book. Their words and support were given graciously and much appreciated. Finally, I want to thank the reader in advance for going on a journey into the evolution of wisdom. My sincerest hope is that it is as enjoyable for you as it has been for me.

Preface

Whatever we do in our lives, I have found that most people want to make an impact, be known for something, or leave their mark on the world. It can be called leaving a legacy. Something of value a person leaves behind for those who follow. Many of those who have come before us, whether family or friends, have left a legacy of some kind.

It is a family belief for my husband and me that we are accountable to those who came before us, and we let our daughters know this as well. The best gift I can bequeath to my daughters is the knowledge of who they are, where they came from, how their mother came to value the world and the people in it, and ultimately, how I seem to "know so much about everything."

Discussing such thoughts with children is important, but in order to protect those valuable nuggets that may be forgotten over time or misunderstood due to their age, I have put together this book about the development of wisdom to help them remember who they are and how some of their values evolved. They may not read this book until their twenties, when they have children of their own, or even later in their lives, but it is my goal to give them a tool from which greatness can emerge.

The impetus, therefore, for this book was to leave something of value behind for my daughters, who are the most precious beings in my world besides my husband. One can leave money, personal effects, and valuable property behind, but the gift of wisdom, love, and a sense of where we come from is something that cannot be taxed away, burned in a fire, or lost on an investment that goes belly-up.

One of the most interesting items left behind in my deceased paternal grandmother's belongings was a paper she had written for her college philosophy class. It was a fascinating journey into how she thought and how she expressed herself. Because she was a private person, I did not know her as well as I knew my maternal grandma. I would consistently enter conversations with her in search of more information, but she would redirect me. Finding the philosophy paper allowed me to see who she was as a person, through her intimate thoughts on various abstract topics.

The stories our ancestors pass down through generations paint pictures of them as real, living, breathing people, so we can better understand our own origins. I understand the importance of our ancestors, even the brief glimpse my paternal grandmother provided into her personal wisdom. We also are inspired and impacted by people in our lives who are not our relations. I want to give my daughters a legacy of my own that captures the value of being a better person in the world, a gift I hope will also benefit all those people whom we and this book come in contact with, as well as generations to come. That is why I wrote this book. My hope is that you will find some wisdom for yourself, your family, and your friends within these pages.

A Word Before You Go, Grandma

The Wisdom of Grandmothers

What is wisdom? Here are a few answers from Merriam-Webster:

- accumulated philosophic or scientific learning
- ability to discern inner qualities and relationships
- good sense
- the teachings of the ancient wise men

I prefer my Grandma Valentine's answer, but that one takes a bit more time to explain:

Grandma liked the word *keen*, and for me that word still conjures up some of the qualities that made her my mentor: the shine of affection in her eyes whenever we talked, her sharp perception of why people behaved the way they did, her ability to pierce to the heart of a matter whenever I needed advice. Grandma was keen on me, and I was keen on her.

Grandma was a thinker, and I was always interested to know her conclusions. I'm still keen on Grandma's wisdom, though she has been gone for more than twelve years.

Lately I find myself thinking a lot about wisdom: what it is and what it isn't, why it's both constant and ever-changing, where it comes from and where it goes, and why some people collect it while others never grasp it. Grandma and I could have talked about this for hours, leaning toward each other in her tiny kitchen, or pressing earnest ears and lips to the phone.

"People will show you what they know through how they act. Just watch them, listen to them."
— Grandma Valentine

The things my grandma taught me might not sound new to you. But that's what amazes me. Maybe your grandma said similar things to help you navigate a difficult situation with a colleague, friend, spouse, or child. But where did *the first* grandma learn it? How do people solve life's challenges? How do they decide which ideas to keep and which to throw away?

I believe we gather wisdom because we're curious about life and yearn for connection. I believe we hold onto wisdom because we cherish the ability to apply knowledge and experience to new situations. I believe we pass wisdom on as a gift because we love people, so we want to save them pain and help them find their path to joy. Grandma knew this, so she passed on her gift to the most willing pupil she could find, the baby of the family: me.

When I think about Grandma, I feel happy. Not that she was a fluffy, hearts-and-flowers, huggy-kissy little old lady. She was a hardworking, sharp-thinking, no-nonsense powerhouse. But working hard and thinking hard made her happy, and she taught me to feel the same way.

When I think about myself—and Grandma taught me the importance of reflection—I feel proud of this: I know how to ask people questions. I often see patterns in human behavior, and those patterns help me understand what to ask. When I make a decision, I truly want what's right for the other person. I believe there's a way to find out what someone else wants and what I want and come up with an answer that lets us both win. I don't need people to think my way. Whether I'm helping someone solve a problem or create an idea, putting that other person in the driver's seat engenders trust. On the other hand, I'm not in true service to others if I merely stroke their egos. I can speak truth to power. At the end of the day, I'm not here to tell anyone what to do, only to ask what I can do. I learned that from Grandma…and Socrates.

"True wisdom comes to each of us when we realize how little we understand about life, ourselves, and the world around us."
— Socrates

At some point, after I've asked all the questions I can ask, I still have to come to a conclusion. I previously served as chair for the board of trustees at the school my two young daughters attend. The school underwent an outdoor renovation in which the process was bumpy. The project brought together people with disparate personalities and values, people who had never worked together before, including people outside of the school community who needed to approve the planned improvements. I had contact with many generous people who donated time and money, but I still witnessed the uncertainty and complications that come when people react before they have all the facts. Grandma's wisdom guided me as I simply listened and asked questions. During this process, one of Grandma's favorite words became my guiding light: humility.

"Humility allows you to hear and listen while making you pleasant and genuinely gracious."
— Grandma Valentine

By the end of the project, the committees spearheading the effort had produced results well beyond what the board expected, and our donors had been more generous than anyone could have imagined. My letter to all who participated was filled with gratitude—and my grandma's wisdom. Here's an excerpt:

Letter from the Board Chair

My grandma always said the most important trait a person could possess was humility. It was her opinion that humility allows people to do all kinds of things such as feel true and deep appreciation, express sincere gratitude, understand how fortunate we are and find true joy in ourselves and the world. She lived through some pretty tough times: WWI, the Great Depression, WWII, the Korean War, the Vietnam War, the Cold War, just to name a few. She shared her recollection of these times with me which is how I developed my love of history, but more importantly, my understanding of why she believed in the value of humility. During some of these times, she had nothing, but she never felt sad about it. Humility allowed her to look deep and find goodness.

Her focus on humility was something I heard and witnessed throughout my childhood and into adulthood and it is the lens I prefer to look through today. When I look through this lens with respect to our School, I see everything that is done in our community by the teachers, the administrators, the parents, the children, the grandparents and those who support us from outside our community. There have been so many great accomplishments this past year that could not have happened without deep dedication, expertise, thoughtfulness and time from all corners of our community and beyond. You will see many of these accomplishments mentioned in this report. It is humbling to be part of such a great community where we share similar goals and desires for our children and their futures...

I believe Grandma would have been proud of my letter. I like to think she "read" it. During one of our last conversations we concluded that our spirits live on after death. We had that conversation during a special weekend together. That was the one time Grandma let me turn the tables and offer *my* wisdom to *her*. It was as if she were passing the torch before she left.

A Last Visit With Grandma

Several years ago, when I was in my early thirties, my aunt and my mother asked if I would stay with Grandma Valentine for the weekend. Grandma was almost ninety and still living independently, but even though she was still sharp and capable, she was almost completely blind. She lived in a duplex, and my Aunt June lived in the unit next door. Between June and my mother, they made Grandma's meals, ran her errands, and looked after her safety and medical needs. But on this particular weekend, they were heading to northern Michigan to open up the family farmhouse for the season, and they didn't want to leave Grandma alone.

I typically worked weekends for my consulting firm, and it was work I loved. But I also loved spending time and talking with my grandma. My grandma was a joy. I found her engaging to talk to, sometimes for hours, even more so at the tender age of ninety, for she was one who never stopped growing in wisdom. She was always eager to listen, analyze, and serve up deep, well-thought-out advice like no one else I knew. Most of her advice required me to come to my own conclusions, and I appreciated the opportunity to be her wisdom apprentice.

So I surprised my firm by announcing that their weekend worker would be leaving at 5:00 p.m. sharp on Thursday and would be out of communication for the weekend. Several people looked surprised. We had just engaged a remarkable client whose project I was excited to work on. One of my firm's partners gave me such a questioning look that I shared my plans to spend the weekend with my grandma. After I told him a bit about my grandma, he said something to the effect of, "That's so sweet." I thought about my grandma, who had inspired me to be a tough professional, and realized she would have laughed if she had heard him call either of us "sweet."

When 5:00 p.m. hit, I left my briefcase behind and grabbed my overnight bag and my key to Grandma's house. The key ring was a gift from my Aunt June, and it had a big G medallion, G for "Grandma." When others saw the G they assumed it stood for my name, Gabrielle. I loved that because it was my little secret (mine and Aunt June's) that it stood for Grandma. It would remind me of our special weekend for years to come.

I took the Metro to Villa Park in the west suburbs of Chicago. Villa Park is a town full of little look-alike boxes built in the fifties and sixties, old-model cars, and an Elks' lodge where blue-collar workers still talk union talk. My uncle was a member there. The walk from the local train station was just a few blocks. My heart grew lighter with each step.

With my G clutched in my hand like a precious jewel, I hurried through the gate to the back door. Nobody used the front door at Grandma's. My mom and aunt had left earlier, and I was concerned that it was almost six o'clock and my grandma was probably hungry for dinner. Although I had a key, I gave a soft tap-tap-tap at the door. It was still Grandma's house and I didn't want to startle her, or make her feel less than queen of her humble castle. "Grandma? It's Gabrielle." Tap-tap-tap. "Grandma?" I waited in protracted silence. She walked slowly and I didn't want to rush her by acting impatient.

When she appeared in the doorway she gave me a firm smile, one that told me without any fuss that I belonged here. With that signal of welcome, I hurried to unlock the door so she would not have to wrestle with it. I slowed my gait to hers as I followed her into her little kitchen.

I spoke in a booming voice to make sure she could hear my words and enthusiasm. "Hi, Grandma! How are you?"

She responded softly, "I'm fine, fine, fine," but quickly changed the subject to me: "How was the trip? Did it take long? How was your day?" Grandma rarely allowed a conversation to center too long on her. It was her kind, self-deprecating way that suggested that everyone else in her world was far more important than herself.

"Let's see what Aunt Junie has left for you," I said, opening the fridge. My aunt always pre-made homemade meals for Grandma and then refrigerated or froze them. We don't do convenience foods in our family. If we want to show our love, we have to make it from scratch. As work-oriented people, we place special value on the effort behind a homemade meal.

Grandma and I caught up and laughed while I warmed up the dinner. I'm sure June made something tasty, but it was partly lost on us because we were distracted by the joy of reconnecting. I brought Grandma up to speed on the exciting project I was working on. We talked about the joy I felt at having more control over my life, because I was no longer just another face in corporate America but instead a valued member of a consulting team.

She asked about my then-boyfriend, Dylan. She was pleased that he was ambitious yet also made time for me, that he treated me like a lady but also respected me as an individual with my own dreams and intellect. I never doubted she would approve of him. (Later he had one brief opportunity to meet her, and I was right: she approved.) This part of the conversation reminded her of my grandpa, the family dreamer who was completely devoted to her. She admitted she still missed him every day, even three years after his passing.

My aunt knew that her mother was lonely, so she had found Grandma a group that provided companionship to seniors: "The Sunshine Something-or-others." Although Grandma appreciated the gesture, and although it was a caring organization, we both had to laugh, because when the Sunshine Ladies phoned or stopped by, the conversations weren't exactly stimulating. They weren't prepared to discuss much more than friendly small talk: "What about this weather?" "How are your daughters?" and "How are you feeling?" But my Grandma was a deep individual with all her faculties, except eyesight. Those well-intentioned women just weren't as well-informed as Grandma about what was going on in the world.

I knew she enjoyed having someone around she could talk to about politics, the way Illinois seemed to be switching from a red state to a blue, and what kind of policy changes that meant. If we disagreed, all the more interesting! But disagreement rarely turned to argument. Each of us respected the unique perspective the other brought to the table.

I washed the dishes, not bothered by her lack of a dishwasher because this way we could have more visiting time. We stayed up talking in the kitchen until I was surprised to see that it was eleven. I was no night owl, and I knew there was no need to be shy about admitting I'd hit a wall. "The couch is calling my name, Grandma."

She lived in a small house: 1,000 square feet, two bedrooms, one bath. Grandma and Grandpa had long used the second bedroom as a dining room to accommodate our countless family holidays and celebrations, back when Grandpa was still alive and Grandma could still see. The improvised 12-by-12-foot dining room was intimate verging on tight, but had always suited our small family just fine. It felt like home, and that was enough. The living room was just that: not a showplace that gathered dust, but a room where friends and family shared their lives. When I was a girl, the couch's end tables always held covered bowls filled with toffees and hard candy. Those candy dishes were the first place my brothers and I visited when we came over. That was okay with Grandma. She liked our excitement at visiting her, even if it started with candy. The candy was a traditional expression of the love we shared, a sign of welcome from her to us, and a symbol that we always had a place in her home.

On this weekend, the living room became my bedroom. My aunt had laid out bedding, and Grandma sat down in her favorite easy chair so we could keep talking as I made up the couch. Then, unable to let go of our time together, I sat down on it to talk a little more.

We were both thorough analysts of human behavior and how it impacted every facet of our lives: family, friendships, work, play, and politics. We did not engage in gossip, though we were unafraid to level strong criticism at human failings in general. We were also compassionate in realizing the challenges others faced, and willing to admit weakness in ourselves. We were excited about the ability of people to overcome obstacles in inspiring ways. Although our thought processes were similar, I recognized generational differences in our views. But I appreciated learning about the different life circumstances that had shaped her ideas. I felt it gave more depth to my understanding of the world, of what in life is timeless and what is fleeting.

One thing was clear, we operated from the same base of values. We were both reflections of values that had taken root in Germany centuries before, and that had traveled with our ancestors in steerage on a freighter from Gdansk to America in the late 1800s. Hunger, cold, and sleeplessness typified their journey. But their values kept them inspired: the values of hard work, no excuses, and no time spent on self-pity that would distract from the business of survival and the dream of a better life. Families are amazing organizations from that standpoint. Grandma and Grandpa Valentine had never told me, "Here is what's important," but their daily behavior and expectations taught me what to value: honesty, lending a hand, never expecting something for nothing, accepting life as it comes, and taking joy in the privilege of work. Even in my early thirties, I understood that this was the greatest inheritance Grandma could ever leave me, something passed on for generations: *the legacy of wisdom.*

As the night wore on, Grandma began to speak more about herself than usual, revealing that she was suffering from painful isolation. Most of her family and friends had passed away, leaving her alone with the uncertainty posed by looming mortality. Her mother had raised two sets of three children, having remarried after her first husband died. My grandma, Alice Valentine, was the oldest child of the second set, all girls. The first three siblings had passed away, and she was only on speaking terms with one of her remaining two sisters. All of her friends were gone. But she didn't linger on the subject for long.

Somehow Grandma and I managed to wash our faces, brush our teeth, and slip into pajamas without a break in our conversation. Finally I confessed, "Okay, Grandma, you know I love talking with you, but now it's really time for me to sleep or I'll drop before your eyes!" First I helped her to her bed. It was just twenty feet away, but I didn't want her to fall if I could help it. I fell asleep the moment my head hit the pillow. But not for long.

I was startled out of deep sleep by a panicked voice. "Gabrielle! Gabrielle!" Grandma's voice, so quiet earlier that I had leaned forward to hear her, was now loud and crackling with alarm. I looked at the digital clock on the end table: it was 1:14 a.m. I jumped to my feet and sprinted down the short hall to her bedroom, terrified that my grandma was in some sort of fatal trouble: A stroke? A heart attack? A fall on the way to the bathroom? When I reached the doorway of her room, my heart galloping with confusion, I stopped short. Grandma had swung her legs to the edge of the bed and was waving her arms in the dark, preparing to feel her way out of her bedroom. I didn't move a muscle, because I didn't want to spook her with my unexpected presence. One of her flailing hands struck me, but at first she didn't seem to notice.

When the moonlight streaming through the nearby kitchen window touched her, I could see that her face was paralyzed with fear. The odd thing was that this nearly blind woman was clearly staring up at something past my head, but when I turned to look nothing was there. She slowly came to her feet, wavering a bit, and I reached out to protect her from a fall.

I kept my voice soft in direct contrast to her raised pitch. Such a change from earlier. "Are you okay, Grandma? I'm here. It's Gabrielle." I ever so slowly reached for her hand. She grabbed my hand and held it tightly. Gently, I wrapped my other arm around her shoulder. She was only four foot ten and it was all too easy for me to wrap my petite five foot two frame around her as I tried to offer physical warmth and reassurance. But her gaze was still puzzled. I was surprised to feel a reserve of strength and courage well up inside me. Grandma's advice and encouragement had always been there to prop me up through difficulties. Now I was ready to return the favor. I cautiously guided her the three feet into the kitchen, where we sat knee-to-knee, face-to-face, and I asked what was wrong.

"I'm scared," she admitted, her voice now shrunken smaller than a child's.

"Scared of what, Grandma?" I asked.

"I'm scared of dying and I feel so alone."

In a family that keeps deep emotions out of sight rather than burden others, Grandma's revelation rocked me to the core. She had always been strong, resolute, and confident, never visibly rattled. We were a family of doers who believed all of life's challenges could be managed. I had no vocabulary, verbal or physical, to deal with this. But I had love, and I was willing to learn on the spot. Grandma's wisdom had taught me that rising to an unfamiliar occasion was doable so long as I relied on all my experiences to give me the instinctive answer.

How do you help someone cope with something so primal as the fear of death? To dismiss it as something that happens to everyone, to lie and say she was not going to die, or to tell her God would welcome her, would skirt the issue of her immediate anxiety. My grandma had been living with a fear so great it was causing sleepless nights. The only solution I could think of was to acknowledge her fear, and assure her that I would support her through it.

"Dying is scary," I said. "But I'm here and you have family around you at all times. We'll help you." I spoke slowly to give her a chance to absorb each word. Time seemed to be moving in slow motion and the air in the tiny kitchen felt heavy.

I doubt Aunt June knew about Grandma's anxiety, even though she lived next door. It felt clear that Grandma was confiding in me something she had never before spoken to a living soul. I knew that she was grateful her daughters were such loyal caregivers and that she didn't want to cause them additional worry or work. Still, she had to talk to someone, and the circle of loved ones near her age had mostly passed away. Her loneliness was not just a feeling, it was her reality. And I was the only one left who understood Grandma well enough to talk to her about it.

I made some weak tea, the way Grandma liked it, and brought the tin of butter cookies to the tiny rectangular table, where we huddled around one corner. We remained silent for a while, gathering our thoughts. I was determined that we identify every aspect of her fear, so we could come up with meaningful strategies for her to cope with it. I strongly feel that the best way to defeat fear is with a plan. Fear left unbridled can be poison to the heart and mind. Grandma was the one who had given me the tools to deal with this moment: we both understood that analyzing and resolving a situation requires extracting emotion so you can understand the facts, but then putting the emotion back in so that you can fully evaluate the potential impact of your decisions.

When we began to talk she, too, spoke slowly, as careful as me in picking her words. After all, I had learned that skill from her. First, we agreed that her fear was real, even if it produced irrational thoughts or behaviors. Second, we realized that the fear of death was preying on her situation as an elderly woman living alone, filling her with questions like: When? How? Will I be reunited with my husband Jimmy and others who have passed before me? Although the hope of seeing Grandpa again was comforting, it did not stop the fear, because of her third issue: the process of crossing over itself scared her because it was a journey she would make alone.

I could tell it helped her to talk to me about it. As I listened, my sense of duty to her was profound. My only regret was that I would return to work on Monday and would not be around to help her face the dark path ahead. Even though my mom and aunt were faithful caretakers who always made themselves available to her, being emotionally available was another story. Grandma had never had the deep conversations with them that she shared with me. They were her daughters, which creates a different connection. Grandma was too wise to try to change that.

Our bond was possible partly because of the generation that separated us. It was not mired in the remembered trials and tribulations of child rearing. When Grandma and the grandkids spent time together it had always been finite, and the grandchildren had always tried to be on their best behavior, so it was easier for Grandma and me to enjoy each other as people. Our relationship was a kinder and more patient relationship because it had developed differently. My mother's responsibility was to take care of her mother's health, and my responsibility was to hold my grandmother's hand and listen to her thoughts and fears about death.

My Grandma was what my family calls a "me-selfer." She spent most of her life so independent it was hard to imagine that this pillar of strength might need anyone, even though she was almost completely blind. Of course she had emotional needs, and she was wise enough to share them with the one person she felt most comfortable sharing them with: me. She had taught me empathy, so she knew I could use my imagination to build a bridge of understanding between us. She knew I would compassionately listen and quietly support her, as she had done for me when I had needed her. So I took her hands and told her that she could always call me and share her fears with me anytime, day or night.

That was enough.

We sat holding hands while the words continued to ease their way out of her. We broke contact now and then for a sip of tea or bite of a cookie, and then I returned my hands to hers with gentle touches of comfort, as we remained that way into the wee hours, knee-to-knee. I was not going to leave her, not for a moment, until she told me it was okay.

That night Grandma gave me an unexpected gift to carry into my old age: "I see lights a lot," she said, "and I don't know what they are." She also said Grandpa often spoke to her in her dreams. She was a rational thinker, and she tried to sort through which parts of these experiences felt real and which felt like dreams. "They don't feel like dreams. They feel as if they come from a different place, and they scare me." I suggested that we accept the possibility that Grandpa was indeed trying to comfort her and assure her, as he had done during their sixty-six-year marriage. "He's probably just trying to let you know that he's waiting for you and you don't need to worry."

We agreed that one of the most beautiful ways to overcome her fear of death was to think about sweet memories of her life. So we reminisced together, calling up old memories. It worked well. By the time I tucked her into her bed, her firm smile was back and it was daybreak.

She later continued to take private walks down memory lane on her own. Sometimes she shared memories with me during our phone calls. I'm sure she did a little praying too, another strategy we discussed. Months later, I lost the most precious person in my life, but I retained the gift of knowing that I had helped her find her way to death with a sense of peace.

Grandma taught me more than anyone I've known about the basic principles that guide me in life. She taught me wisdom, and before she passed away she gave me an opportunity to practice what I'd learned. Now I'm ready to pass it on.

What Would Grandma Valentine Say?

Wisdom is knowing and doing the right thing, based on a keen understanding of human emotions and behaviors and the use of experience to develop a better understanding of life.

A Step Toward Wisdom

Here's what I think wisdom is: the culmination of the human abilities of compassion, knowledge, logic, and humility, used in combination to assess situations, make decisions, and take action.

2

Filling the Wisdom Toolbox

"The important thing is not to stop questioning.
Curiosity has its own reason for existing."
– Albert Einstein

The Road to Wisdom is Paved with Connections

Those with a better ability to analyze situations have that gift primarily because they've developed more connections in the brain. We start making those connections as children, though it takes a long time to figure out how to apply them. That's why it's good to encourage children to ask questions, and why it's so important to encourage them to take the risk to try new things and not be afraid of making mistakes. Each time a child tries something new, whether she succeeds or fails, she increases the number of connections in her brain, and therefore increases her ability to analyze future situations and make better choices.

Although genes play a role in intelligence, that role is often overrated. Several scientific studies have shown that people can actually increase their IQ scores through the effort they put into learning new things. In 2011, researchers at University College London reported astonishing changes in teen intelligence quotient tests over a four-year period.

The study, published in the journal *Nature*, followed 33 adolescents who were between twelve and sixteen years old when the study started. Over the four years of the study, their IQ scores fluctuated as many as 20-plus points.

My Grandma Valentine used to start many conversations with the enthusiastic phrase "Life is interesting." She definitely would have used that phrase to refer to the human ability to increase one's IQ. It's certainly a validation of her own efforts because, even though she only had an eighth-grade education, she sought information all her life, primarily through talking to people and reading. Grandpa would spend hours reading *National Geographic* and *Scientific American* magazine articles to her, although she also knew how to read. I believe she was a brilliant woman, and her desire for knowledge was a visceral part of her being. It all started with her curiosity about people and life, and her willingness to keep asking questions and seeking answers.

There is a definite link between curiosity and wisdom. Psychologists Todd B. Kashdan and Michael F. Steger have argued that highly curious people recognize the growth potential of challenging events. They came to that conclusion after studying 97 students for their 2007 paper, Curiosity and Pathways to *Well-being and Meaning in Life: Traits, States, and Everyday Behaviors*. They ended up confirming the findings of many previous studies: that human curiosity motivates exploration of the self and the world, which expands one's knowledge and skills, which improves quality of life.

To paraphrase Kashdan and Steger: gathering experiences, reflecting, and then seeking more experiences leads to a greater sense of meaning and satisfaction in one's life. As for me, I would take that a step further and assert that wisdom is the exercise of infusing our experiences with meaning. In other words, I believe we choose to make the links that we need in order to create meaning for ourselves. In any case, significant levels of curiosity must exist to allow for the development of wisdom.

"To have an education is very important but to always seek knowledge is even more important."
— Grandma Valentine

Grandma's curiosity prompted her to continue creating new links in her brain throughout her adult life, even toward the end. She was excited when I shared my new experiences, especially as her ability to collect experiences became much more restricted in her nineties. Her thirst for connections and experiences is probably one reason she didn't suffer much mental decline in her later years. Wisdom is largely based on the ability to apply our past knowledge and experience to new situations, so it also requires a sharp memory.

Plenty of research has shown that lifelong learners like my grandma have a lower risk of developing memory loss. Brain researchers have discovered that as some of the brain's neural pathways die off a healthy brain continues to makes new ones. This process of building new brain highways is called "neuralplasticity." The brain wants to think, so it strives to do so any way it can. This is why neuralplasticity researchers from the University of California at San Francisco Medical

School say that the solution to memory loss is brain exercise. They've discovered that when we learn complex new things, we create more neural highways.

But the brains with the most connections always get their initial boost in childhood.

Putting is like wisdom – partly a natural gift and partly the accumulation of experience.
– Arnold Palmer

Grandma Grew Up An Outsider

My grandma was a first-generation American, born in 1910 to German immigrants. Grandma's mother married twice, because her first husband passed away, so she had two sets of three children. Since my grandma was the eldest child of the second set, she held a unique place in the dual family: she was both an eldest child and a middle child. According to popularly held beliefs about birth order, her experiences were those of both the leader and the one who struggles to be acknowledged. So, from the beginning, my grandma had the advantage of seeing things from multiple viewpoints.

Like many German immigrants at the turn of the last century, Grandma's family had settled in Chicago, where the cold climate must have felt familiar. Many of the immigrants who arrived with them had little or no education, but they had a desire and eagerness to work hard to achieve freedom and start fresh in a new country with so much promise. Ironically, although my grandma was the smartest among the second set of sisters, she was the least educated. Grandma used to say, "I always took care of Bernice and Irene. That was my job for the family." Bernice was her younger sister, and Irene was the youngest. One of the ways she helped take care of both of them was by quitting school so she could help her mother watch them and do the housework. As a result, my grandma only received an eighth-grade education. Whether that's what she wanted or not, it was what was expected of her and her older siblings. Thanks to the sacrifices of their older sister, the two youngest benefitted by finishing high school.

Our duty is to be useful, not according to our desires but according to our powers.
— Henri-Frédéric Amiel

My grandma never complained about having to quit school. She wasn't the type to dwell on what might have been. Instead she always accepted that the past is the past and you work with what you have in the present. Still, I recall a fleeting look of longing when we discussed my own educational plans. But that look held more hope than jealousy, signaling to me the high regard she had for education. She took tremendous joy in knowing that I was going on to pursue college. If she had been born in 1968, as I was, I suspect she would have been the sort of woman to earn a PhD and go on to greatness, perhaps as a scientific researcher because of her great curiosity, or a political leader because of her deep and vast understanding of people.

By the time Grandma was twenty, the Great Depression had taken hold of the entire country. Back then, as Grandma put it, "Everyone did any kind of work they could get their hands on because jobs were hard to find." It was especially difficult for new immigrants to the United States to find work, because they were treated like second-class citizens. They had to work hard not only to establish themselves and their families, but also to gain respect as potential new citizens of the United States. But Grandma was the type who sought to learn from her experience, and being treated like nothing because she came from a family of new immigrants was a lesson she would never forget. She grew up committed to valuing people for who they were, and not what they were. It was one of the first brain connections she made as an observer of life, and she passed that wisdom on to me.

I Grew Up Seeking Connections

I was only two years old when my parents began divorce proceedings. Their marriage had a tragic nature to it. My mom and dad are two well-educated, interesting, sweet people. They met in high school, when they were two spirited kids who didn't have the experience to realize they weren't compatible for a life together raising three children. They had separate dreams, expectations, and needs. That disparity made for volatile arguments and deep frustration between a couple who were otherwise vivacious and friendly as individuals. To further complicate matters, my mother was from a blue-collar immigrant family and my father was from a well-to-do socialite family. So their two families were riddled with misunderstandings that compounded their marital problems. They divorced when I was very small, but that didn't spare me from family strife.

Unfortunately my mother entered into a rocky second marriage. So I didn't have the most calm and peaceful home environment growing up. But I've discovered that if you have at least one adult in your life who offers you a sense of continuity and sanity, it can make up for a lot of dysfunction. Grandma was that person for me.

I watched the way Grandma accepted my mother's choices and didn't waste a lot of time lecturing her or saying, "I told you so." At least, not in front of her grandchildren. Even if she didn't approve of the men her daughter chose, she knew that she could not make those choices for her. She was proud that her daughter had at least gone as far as possible with her education, earning two master's degrees, the type of education that had never been an option for Grandma. She understood that each of us has our own path to follow, and that not everyone's path can be rooted in wisdom.

"By three methods we may learn wisdom: first, by reflection, which is noblest; second, by imitation, which is easiest; and third by experience, which is the bitterest."
– Confucius

Wisdom is not just about having experience, but also about paying attention to what your experience is telling you. If you want to gain wisdom from experience, you have to ask more questions of others and of yourself. You have to take an interest not only in *what* happens to you, but in *why* it's happening. And you have to take an interest not only in what led you down the path you're on, but also what led other people to share that path with you.

Every situation, positive or negative, is an opportunity to apply your curiosity and gather knowledge. That requires stopping and asking questions, of both yourself and the other people involved. The knowledge you gain doesn't become wisdom until you apply it the next time a similar situation arises. To turn knowledge into wisdom, you must pause and analyze each new situation in terms of what you've previously learned and experienced, maintaining clarity and intellectual honesty. This requires applying both logic and imagination. Your logic will help you add up clues based on past experiences, but your imagination will allow you to make predictions about things that might happen, even if they haven't happened before and direct knowledge is not available.

The Old Man Next Door

When I was three years old I snuck out of the house, unbeknownst to my mother, and went off on an adventure. I went pretty far for a three-year-old on her own: next door. Like Grandma, I was always curious to discover new things and learn about people. At three, this translated into rocking a big chair back and forth on a porch and asking a million questions of Mr. Juhnke, a retired humanities professor from the local college. I thought he must be more than a hundred years old, though he was probably more like eighty-five, but he never seemed to tire of my questions.

My mother used to tell me that my love of conversation wore her out. By age three, I was already stringing together run-on sentences that could go on for minutes. It turns out there's a scientific basis for the desire to talk about ourselves, which we spend about 40 percent of every conversation doing. According to a 2012 study published in the Proceedings of the National Academy of Sciences, whenever humans engage in self-disclosure it leads to biochemical activity in the reward centers of the brain, the same areas that respond when we eat or have pleasurable physical relations. Researchers Diana I. Tamir and Jason P. Mitchell of Harvard University's psychology department found that people were even willing to give up a monetary reward in return for the opportunity to talk about themselves.

It wasn't only the sound of my own voice I was after. For me, the big reward of my conversations with Mr. Juhnke was obtaining the answers to why everything and everyone in the world existed. My mother didn't have quite enough patience, or mostly, time, to answer all my questions. Mr. Juhnke did.

So it became a habit. The first couple of times, I disappeared from our house in the early morning when everyone was still asleep. My mother panicked when she woke to find me missing. She raced around the house calling my name, peering under every bed and in every closet. When she finally found me on the neighbor's porch, sporting my fancy undershirt and ruffled underwear, she admonished me not to bother him. My mother, in her own wisdom, appreciated the fact that he was a very private man. But I'm glad he told her, "But I'm really enjoying getting to know my little visitor. She's not bothering me at all. It's a pleasure."

In one fell swoop he taught me four lessons that would set me on the path to wisdom: 1) showing a genuine interest in others makes them more interested in us, 2) curiosity is good and should be encouraged, 3) stepping outside our comfort zone yields rewards, and 4) even the smallest kindnesses are worthwhile in connecting us to other people. I'll never forget that sweet man and his extra rocking chair.

Those early connections formed the neural pathways that would establish one of my brain's strongest attributes for life: my desire to learn from other people. Thankfully I use shorter sentences now, stopping to take a breath now and then, and to make sure I'm truly listening—even to the pauses.

In my conversations with Mr. Juhnke, I wasn't merely pursuing a conversation, or attention, or escape—though I certainly enjoyed those aspects of our visits. No, I wanted to know whatever it was that my neighbor knew, experienced, and felt in this world. I wanted to find out whatever information and connection he might have to offer. It was my first awareness of other people being distinct from me, living lives of their own, having separate thoughts, dreams, and feelings. I was already on a journey in pursuit of wisdom.

Wonder is the beginning of wisdom.
– Socrates

A Bridge Across the Generations

My Grandma was much older than most of my friends' grandmothers. Although it gave us less time together on this planet, it never bothered me in terms of feeling some vast generation gap between us. If anything, it only made me curious to learn about all that existed in that gap. I liked having access to someone who had so many more years of experience than I did. It's a value I wish more of us would appreciate and explore while our elders are with us.

There's a tendency in America to value all that is new, but only the old can really give us perspective on what is valuable in both the new and the old, because they've seen it all. Much of what we think of as new is actually something old that they've seen before, just dressed up in a new guise. Grandma taught me that I could save a lot of time and have more fun in life if I learned from past experiences and especially past mistakes, both mine and others'. Her recollections of her own experiences and observations were not only interesting, but also provided broad similarities to some of my own situations. Although I went on to work in corporate America and she ran a Mom-and-Pop business, we both agreed that humans in the workplace behave in similar ways.

My grandma was a grounded person who appreciated the need for balance, and that may be why she and my grandpa fell in love. Because Grandpa Valentine (whom she called "Jimmy") was a dreamer. They complemented each other and gave to each other new ways of doing things and thinking about the world. She helped anchor him, but he gave her wings. Together, they were quite a team.

It was Grandpa Valentine's inspiration to purchase the Dog N' Suds, a great place for hot dogs, root beer, hamburgers, and French fries. My brother's entire kindergarten class once went there on a field trip for free soft-serve cones hand-dipped in chocolate. As a little girl, I thought that such a delicious, laughter-filled place must be the best kind of business to own in the world, but I could still see how tough it was.

My grandma and grandpa hired help, but only teenagers would take that type of job in the seventies. The kids they hired were often unreliable, more interested in having an unearned good time than earning the rewards of hard work. So Grandma and Grandpa ended up doing most of the work. The value of work was part of Grandma's German upbringing, but it still took a toll on both of them. I could see how exhausted and harried they often were. Still, I could also see the personal pride Grandpa took in making his dream a reality, and the loving pride Grandma took in helping her life partner make it happen.

Having seen the way my grandparents worked together gave me a deep understanding of what a solid marriage was all about. A child on the road to wisdom doesn't have to have a perfect life, just access to people who will offer her significant glimpses of what it looks like when relationships work—relationships of all kinds. Watching them work, I saw what it could be like when employees let you down, but I also saw what it could be like when colleagues build you up and when couples pull together.

Despite the many times they struggled to keep their business profitable, and despite how relieved they were the day they sold it, Grandma always focused on taking away positives from their experience running the Dog N' Suds. She realized that ownership is a double-edged sword: the freedom to call your own shots balanced against the need to rely on other people. Grandma never blamed herself when employees showed up late, goofed off, or stole from the till. She knew that the only person she could control was herself. Once she learned the patterns of unreliable employees, she kept her eyes peeled for those patterns in new hires. She couldn't control other people, but she could learn enough about them to help her make better decisions. When it came time for me to join the workforce, she passed on to me what she had learned.

For most of the time I knew my grandparents, they were retired. This was also a benefit to me on the road to wisdom, because they always had plenty of time for us kids, even me and all my questions! They always stayed with us whenever my mom and stepfather went on trips. I took every opportunity to hang by my grandma's side in the kitchen, talking to her in one long run-on sentence until she could distract me with a job to do. Even then Grandma was teaching me about work. I noticed that, although she was always busy, she was content with busy-ness. It was simply as much a part of her as breathing. I was proud when she asked me to help.

Sitting down for afternoon tea was her moment of rest, so it became mine, too. That was when she would listen to my questions. She had a gentle way of listening. When I described something, she would lift her head up as if catching a scent in the air. It was her way of letting me know whether my words were communicating clear meaning to her. One thing I loved about Grandma was that she often answered my questions with questions of her own. In that way, she forced me not only to wonder about how the world worked and why people did what they did, but also to put my brain to work on analyzing how it all fit together. Asking questions was her way of prompting her grandchildren to think and draw our own conclusions.

Those teatimes with Grandma taught me to be careful and intentional with my words, as she was. Grandma started with basic rules of speech. For example, she taught me never to casually throw out phrases like "that was terribly nice of you." "How could something be terrible and nice?" Grandma asked rhetorically. That was a real pet peeve of hers. To this day, I think of her when I put words together, trying to make sure that I use the words that most clearly state what I mean without adding unintended connotations.

Although Grandma appreciated my desire to speak, she was clearly concerned that if I became too busy talking I might not listen carefully. She made it clear to me that listening was the most important part of a conversation. She gently encouraged me not only to listen, but also to observe. "Watch how people say things and see what they do. The words are especially important if they do not match how they are saying things and what they are doing."

She was teaching me some pretty basic communication skills, but few people stop to explain such things to a ten-year-old, and I wish more people would. Remember, the earlier we form those connections, the more time we have to build them. As for me, watching for the differences between what people did and what they said became very meaningful as I headed into middle school. I became more observant and witnessed how often people's words and actions didn't match, and with that I grew very quiet for the first time in my life.

I spent a reflective couple of years until I went to high school. Many of my fellow students in middle school thought I was quiet and shy. However, I was simply taking a long pause from my love of conversation so that I could observe every-thing and everyone around me. To this day, I believe that Grandma's advice helped me survive the perils of middle school, a time when many kids discover that they can make their own choices, and often hurt a lot of other people in the process. Because I paid attention, and steered clear of people whose words and actions didn't match, I escaped a lot of the emotional trauma so many kids experience at that age.

It's one of the gifts of wisdom that I'm trying to pass on to my two daughters, Brooke and Morgan, as they get ready to step into that wider world. These days Americans are focused on "know who you are" and "express who you are," which I think is great. But we can't forget the other piece, which is "find out who *other* people are." To do that, you have to learn when to speak and act, when to listen and observe, and then how to make the connections that put it all together: who you are and what you want, and who everyone else is and how their wants fit with yours.

I'm still working on it. Like Grandma, I'll be working on it all my life.

What Would Grandma Valentine Say?

The first step to gathering wisdom is simply deciding that you want to find it. Gaining wisdom requires one to look, learn, and listen.

A Step Toward Wisdom

I believe wisdom starts when we cultivate a genuine interest in others and the world around us. When we ask interested questions, we begin to understand what people want and why they act the way they do.

3

Using Your Head

*"A good head and a good heart are always a
formidable combination."*
– Nelson Mandela

Keep an Even Keel

We've all experienced a moment when we've lost self-control. Even if it's been years since it happened to you, surely you still see a glimpse of the possibility now and again, especially when you're tired or hungry. Someone does or says something so offensive that your first impulse is to say, "How dare you?" and maybe throw in a few expletives. If you're a normal human, then sometime in your youth you probably did lose control, doing whatever came to mind. Instead of saying, "I'm not sure I understand. Can you explain?" it can seem easier to aggressively confront the other person.

When we learn to maintain our emotional homeostasis, we react to those situations differently. Instead of reacting, we engage in reflecting: both self-reflecting and reflecting back what is going on with the other person. Emotional homeostasis is the state we achieve when our emotional needs feel satisfied and we therefore feel balanced and calm.

People who are effective at maintaining emotional homeostasis have the ability to stay balanced even in situations that
might prompt irrational fear, disgust, hatred, or desolation in
others. We often call such emotions negative, because they
cause us pain or discomfort, but the truth is that so-called
negative emotions have a survival benefit. They help us
avoid dangerous or life-threatening situations, such as a
wild animal, violent person, or rotting food, and they help
us seek safe or life-promoting situations, such as a friendly
group, a potential mate, or healthy food. The problem is that
modern humans have achieved so many advancements in
safe and healthy living that many of our negative emotional
reactions are still set on high alert for ordinary interactions
that don't require it.

Homeostasis is a term derived from two Greek words:
homoios, which means "of the same kind," and *stasis*, which
means "standing still." The concept of homeostasis was
originally developed by Dr. Claude Bernard, a nineteenth-
century French physiologist, who studied the way that the
body reacts to stabilize itself in the face of negative external
stimuli. Later, in 1932, American physiologist Walter Cannon
gave that concept the name homeostasis, and expanded on it
to describe the body's need to maintain a relatively constant
internal environment. Emotional homeostasis refers to
maintaining emotional calm in the face of negative feedback.

When people with well-developed emotional homeostasis
face people who behave negatively or communicate poorly,
they don't typically lose control. Instead, they are able to pause
and remind themselves, "Even though this person is saying or
doing potentially damaging things to me or in my presence,

their behavior probably isn't about me, it's about something else. Even if it is about me, I need more information to understand what it means and what my responsibility is in this situation before I lash out." A person who understands how to maintain emotional homeostasis has a default response to negative input or feedback: "I don't have to react the moment I receive the negative information. I can give my logical brain time to process it without allowing my emotion centers to take over." A person with emotional homeostasis is balanced internally. To the rest of the world he appears unflappable.

Maintaining emotional homeostasis doesn't mean that I'll be a doormat and let people walk all over me, but rather that, if I do find it necessary to defend myself, I'll have time to prepare a better response. When we let other people hold opinions or ideas that feel wrong to us, when we give them the space to think and feel whatever they're thinking and feeling, often they will come to new conclusions on their own, without us having to get embroiled in conflict. On the other hand, if they do decide to hold onto their position, then often it can be best for us not to waste our time engaging in a conflict that will produce no results.

When humans jump on negative input and act on their initial emotional response, their mental state becomes unbalanced at that moment. Once that happens, the brain loses its ability to intake and process new information. In her book *My Stroke of Insight: A Brain Scientist's Personal Journey*, neuroanatomist Jill Bolte Taylor explains that if you wait about ninety seconds for an automatically triggered emotional reaction to pass, that gives your brain time to get past its initial impulse. Then you're able to ask questions that ensure you have better information, process that information, and offer a well-reasoned reaction. This increases your chances of a positive outcome, not just for the other person, but also for yourself.

"A successful man is one who can lay a firm foundation with the bricks others have thrown at him."
– David Brinkley

The only way you can understand a situation fully is if you remain open to receiving new information. If you'd like examples of experts at this skill, think of interviewers like Barbara Walters, Oprah Winfrey, and the late David Brinkley and Mike Wallace. They've interviewed so many people that it's not possible for them to share the same values with all their interview subjects, yet if you've watched their interviews, you've seen that they're consistent in their ability to calmly but persistently probe whoever is in the hot seat. That is emotional homeostasis in action.

Mike Wallace had many such interviews over the course of his sixty-year-plus career. On September 21, 1957, on *The Mike Wallace Interview*, Wallace spoke with Margaret Sanger, one of the early and formidable advocates for birth control. She held beliefs on marriage, the Catholic Church, and over-population that were controversial for the time. She was a nurse by training and prided herself on being motivated by compassion to end suffering and cruelty. However, the means she chose to accomplish her goals pitted her against belief systems that many Americans and American churches held sacred, including their belief in God and a woman's role in building a family. Much of the public engaged in angry knee-jerk reactions toward Sanger that led to the ostracizing of her and her family, and the breakup of her first marriage.

Although Wallace indicated that he didn't share Sanger's views, if you listen to the archived interview I believe you'll find it difficult to detect in which areas he disagreed with her. Wallace maintained emotional homeostasis throughout the twenty-five-minute interview. He challenged her on many points, but did so in a way that demonstrated he was seeking clarification in an effort to better understand her positions.

"I feel fulfilled when we've revealed a person."
— Mike Wallace

If you want to learn as much as possible about what makes others tick, especially those you disagree with, you can achieve that most effectively and efficiently through maintaining your emotional homeostasis. Put another way, when you momentarily set aside your emotions surrounding an event or topic, you set the stage for increased understanding. That's not to say you'll learn to agree with your opponents, but that you'll have a better chance of finding common ground, and even of discovering what you can do in future to improve your chances of gaining ground. Emotional homeostasis is only one subcomponent of wisdom, but it's an important one.

Many experiences cause us to react with painful emotions, emotions we sometimes call "negative," such as anger, sadness, loneliness, or fear. If we allow ourselves to experience these emotions, instead of fighting them, they can help us reflect on our experiences, learn from our mistakes, and promote understanding between people. Negative experiences, and sometimes the pain and discomfort they produce, become our teachers. For example, experiencing the pain that toxic people cause us might teach us how to avoid such people in future, or experiencing how panicking in a crisis can make things worse might teach us how to project calm during a future crisis and improve our chances of achieving a better result.

Remember Kahlil Gibran's quote at the beginning of this book: "Out of suffering have emerged the strongest of souls; the most massive of characters are seared with scars." That's not to suggest that we should hurt ourselves so we can experience suffering, but rather that surviving a difficult experience allows us to file away what we learn for future reference. When we allow suffering to teach us, our chances of survival and growth increase in the future.

Listen for the Takeaways

Sometimes the most old-fashioned wisdom is the most profound. My grandma was one of those who believed in making lemonade out of lemons, and I believe that was her simple but effective secret for maintaining emotional homeostasis. When I look back on disagreements with friends, struggles at school, or professional conflicts with colleagues, they certainly weren't situations I desired. But I followed Grandma's advice and always looked for whatever learning or observation I could take away from the interaction that would be valuable to me in the future, no matter how small.

Whenever I was frustrated with people and wanted to confront them about it, Grandma's advice was, "Don't react. Don't show them how you feel just yet. Think, think, think. Do not react." She taught me to allow situations to unfold, observe them with clarity, and not let my emotional reactions muddy the water. When we do that we not only gain understanding of the situation so we can react peacefully, but we also allow ourselves space to reflect on our own part in things and to find that nugget of value to take away from the situation.

"If you react based on your emotions, you're going to burn bridges. Down the road, you will regret burning bridges."
– Grandma Valentine

I've discovered that when I pause to ask questions, listen, and process all the information, I learn more about other people. Therefore I learn more about everything in life, from family and friendship to business and politics. I receive joy from an exchange of thoughts and viewpoints. I've collected other people's ideas for my entire life in an effort to fully understand the world and the people who share it. My opinions, over time, have been tempered with the kind of flexibility and compassion that allow me to work with others toward positive goals and solutions, even when we might be far apart philosophically, religiously, politically, or culturally.

Here's the starting point I always try to keep in mind for any relationship, whether it's personal or professional: I'm here for the conversation, so I can learn more about you and, in the process, learn more about me. Over the years, those conversations have become building blocks for wisdom, allowing me to analyze what works and what doesn't and to use that information to create guidelines for living. That wisdom all sprang from my conversations with Grandma.

My grandma reached her nineties when I was in my thirties. But we had more than a decade to engage in long philosophical conversations that gave me a key to unlock many conversations I've had with others. When she started our conversations with her simple phrase, "Life is interesting," what she was really saying was, "People are interesting." I can think of no better way to get along with others than by expressing interest in them. Wisdom sometimes appears in one's life after much thought, and sometimes it never appears. Grandma taught me that even those who seem unwise have something to offer, if only I remain a willing student.

Wisdom Starts with Education

Another way to look at emotional homeostasis is that it requires solving problems with your brain, not your heart or gut. That's not to say all three don't play a role: if your heart's not in something, you may not feel enough love or inspiration to continue, and using your intuition or gut-feeling is often another way of allowing all your senses to come together in ways your conscious mind can't. However, when you know how to use your head to evaluate information, you can make better decisions about what your heart and gut tell you.

My grandma exercised her brain by being a student of life, but she also valued formal education. She understood that education was a way to target the delivery of information for specific uses. She encouraged her daughters and grandkids to seek higher education. She was proud when my mom pursued multiple master's degrees and became a director of nursing, and she was proud when I went off to college.

When young people leave home for college, they often see it as an opportunity to break away from the constraints of family rules and standards. I did experience some of that. It's important to break away from family expectations and discover who you are as an individual. However, a wise person also understands that independent people learn to stand on their own by knowing when to reach out to others for guidance. My grandmother had a track record of serving me well as a mentor, and I realized that she wouldn't always be available for me to benefit from her wisdom and experience. So, throughout college, I relied on Grandma's advice more than that of my instructors or counselors. She helped me make many important connections between theory and practice that I still use in conducting business today.

I was in my mid-twenties when I decided to go on to get my MBA. There were two top-notch business schools on my list. I knew it would be difficult to get accepted because my standardized test scores were compromised by my dyslexia. However, I knew that if I applied myself to complete a well-written application, demonstrate my many professional successes and awards, and give a confident and thoughtful personal interview, I could increase my chances.

During my first personal interview, the interviewer treated me with utter disinterest throughout our conversation, as if she had already decided not to admit me. I was devastated. I still had another application and interview to go through for a different school, and I was terribly nervous because I could not figure out where I went wrong in the first interview. I called the Admissions Office to fish for feedback but had no success. My confidence began to ebb, and I feared that my dream of attending a top business school might slip away. So I called Grandma.

I recounted my application process to her. I explained that, in an effort to create the best essay possible, I had asked for input from several professional, intelligent friends, colleagues, and family members who were excellent writers.

Without much more information than that, Grandma quickly deduced where I'd gone wrong. "You relied too much on other people's input."

"Are you sure, Grandma? Maybe you should read the essay."

"I don't need to read it. Everything you're telling me makes it clear. You were so eager to get into that school that you let other people edit all your passion and ambition right out of the essay, allowing their personalities and expertise to take over."

She advised that, for my next essay, I spend more time looking inward and then put on the page the best of what I found within. I was worried that whatever was in me might not be what they were looking for. Grandma told me there was no point in worrying about that, because there was no way to know exactly what they were looking for. She assured me that putting the real me out there was my best bet, because that's something few people are brave enough to do.

Right after I got off the phone, I wrote my essay for The University of Chicago's business school, while Grandma's inspiration and confidence in me were fresh. I spent hours sequestered inside on a beautiful day even though I was tempted to go outside. I emerged with a rough draft I was proud of. This time I only gave my final draft to one writer— my brother, Tim—and requested he only correct errors of grammar and usage. I made only those corrections and, without showing it to anyone else, enclosed the essay with my other application materials and mailed it. I waited so long for a response that I again began to doubt myself. Was I just not cut out for the business world?

Finally the school offered me an interview. I met with the director of admissions, and I could immediately sense a difference in this interview. She seemed to be truly interested in knowing my personal story. The atmosphere was so different from that of my previous interview at the other school that it was disarming. I knew at that moment that my grandmother was right. There was no way to know exactly what this woman wanted in a business school candidate. But I had confidence in who I was as a person, and I had a deep desire to make it in the business world.

A few months after the interview, I received an acceptance letter from The University of Chicago's Booth School of Business. I was so excited I called Grandma. She was happy for me but surprisingly calm. She never asked me a single question about my essay, and never gave me a "you see, I told you" speech. Instead, she reminded me that it was very important for me to know why I had decided to attend business school, why I had selected The University of Chicago, and what I had done to be accepted. She was asking me to reflect on my experience of success and own it, so that I could use that lesson in the future.

One of the values I learned in business school was a value that my grandma had already taught me: that we don't need to know all the details of every situation to make an informed decision. What we need is to use our previous experience and education to assess the information provided, and then fill in the blanks with sensible assumptions where necessary. That was one reason for attending business school, to develop a mental information bank. Our professors taught us to read situations and then combine imagination with experience to anticipate outcomes. Many top business schools require at least two years of work experience to create practical reference points for theories learned in class.

It was similar to what Grandma taught me when I was a girl. She always told me that, so long as I paid attention to life's lessons as they came, I would have the information stored away to draw upon later. Whenever I called to ask her advice about a tough choice I faced, she made a lot of astute guesses about the experience I was going through, based on very little information. "I don't need all the information," Grandma said, "because I've learned a lot about human nature in my life. Styles change, but human behavior doesn't change all that much."

Between my professors and my grandma, I grew excited about the notion of using incomplete information to put together a complete puzzle. In fact, having too much information sometimes seemed to stymie creativity. Although logical input and bottom-line results are important to factor in, the imaginative piece is where the big innovations happen. Grandma had been training me to have the mindset of a creator without my even realizing it.

I was proud to see my grandmother's beaming face in the crowd when I graduated from business school. She was almost completely blind by that time, but I knew she was hanging on every word in the ceremony. She recognized my degree as a real accomplishment, not something I had pursued just because it was expected or because I wanted to earn more money, but because I was genuinely interested in gaining knowledge so that I could go on to apply it. She was also relieved that I had a way to look after myself, because she had seen my mother go through two difficult marriages and she didn't want me to rely on marriage for fulfillment. Although she had been blessed with a loving marriage to a well-suited partner, she knew that marriage was no guarantee of security or happiness. She was glad that I had enough education to be self-reliant.

Education is Work, and Work is Education

Grandma said education should come first. She did not only mean formal education. She also meant the overarching idea of gathering knowledge from all we learn and experience. In that vein, although education prepares us for work, work can also give us an education.

I've worked since I was eleven. My first "real" job was working as a tennis monitor for the local recreation district. I also went door-to-door with flyers selling my babysitting and pet-sitting services throughout our large neighborhood. I earned a lot more money than my typical peers. My early work experience taught me to connect effort with financial reward, an important lesson in the head-over-heart aspect of wisdom. I did not renounce having fun in my youth, and playtime too was an important part of my development, but my early work experiences taught me many valuable lessons.

One lesson I learned as a young worker was gratitude for what my mother provided through hard work, instead of a sense of entitlement to life's needs and comforts without effort. Another lesson was the self-reliance we develop when we learn that we can provide for ourselves through our own efforts. I was able to use the money I made to buy myself some of the extras I wanted, which helped me extrapolate what a good work ethic would mean for my future. Another lesson was how job experience would improve my abilities and opportunities for the next job. The most important lesson I learned from my earliest jobs was the self-esteem that comes from accomplishment. So, even though sometimes my heart wanted to play games, giggle with girlfriends, or watch TV, my head chose to first honor the cause-and-effect of effort and reward.

I landed my first regular job at a fast-food restaurant when I was only fourteen. By the time I was fifteen, management entrusted me with more responsibility: they made me a crew trainer, put me in charge of closing up, and relied on me to speak Spanish to non-English-speaking employees. I had taken Spanish classes since middle school, a skill that served me well.

I believe I moved up the ladder of success a lot faster throughout my working life because I built a reservoir of positive work experiences when I was young. For example, as a crew trainer I learned leadership skills that later came in handy in business management, and as a Spanish-speaker I later became a valuable leader for one company's entry into Mexico's market.

By the time I finished high school, I had a leg up to college because I had already advanced beyond fast-food service to performing office work as an accounting clerk and legal secretary. Many young people have trouble finding and holding that type of work because teens tend to let their emotions run their lives: a boyfriend breaks up with them and they call in sick, or they decide it will be fun to party until 2:00 a.m. but are unable to pay the price when it comes time to wake up at 7:00 a.m., or they have a strict manager they disagree with and they blurt their anger without thinking it through. With my grandmother's help, I had learned to weigh my needs against those of other people, and to consider the possible outcomes of my actions.

I built a positive work record by primarily doing three things:

1) I listened to other people.
2) I did what I said I was going to do.
3) I did not let my emotions run my behavior.

Focusing on those three things allowed me to create a network of professional support, which was helpful when it came time to work my way through college. Because I'd spent my high school years nurturing positive connections with responsible, well-networked adults, I was able to land a job in the legal department of a title insurance company at nineteen. In that job, I functioned as a trusted right-hand woman to the attorney administering my section.

The working world taught me that wisdom is not a possession but a practice. As such, it does not require white hair, although I hope I will continue to improve in the practice of wisdom until I have hair as white as my departed grandma's.

The Head Knows What the Heart Needs

Whether the knowledge and experience we gather along the way comes from work or school or life itself, it's all part of a total education that can help us make big decisions, particularly about career, marriage, and family. Grandma was lucky to meet the right guy when she was young, but she said that if she hadn't she would have waited—even back in 1931. She knew that modern life gave me even more flexibility: in this country, women born in my generation and after have not had to rely as much on luck in seeking a partner. New social norms, women's rights, and the acceptance of women in the workplace allow us more time, more choices, and more freedom to choose whether or not to marry at all. After witnessing my mother's marriages, I didn't feel pressure to marry. It would be great if it happened, but I was cautious not to expect it.

"Take your time to find the right person," Grandma told me. "Not just someone you're excited about right now, but someone who will work well with you in making difficult decisions and going through hard times."

"Don't worry. I'm like you, Grandma," I said. "I'm not looking to marry just anyone. If I don't find the right person, I don't need to be married just for the sake of being married."

Grandma believed deciding to marry would require a lot of the same mental processes I would use in deciding to enter a business partnership. I needed to consider a potential mate in terms of chemistry, yes, but also in terms of values, long-term compatibility, decision-making skills, conflict resolution, and more. I needed someone who would understand how to maintain emotional homeostasis during tough times, and who would help me do the same.

In fact, I did get engaged when I was twenty-six, but I broke it off. Why? "He didn't want to get married enough for me to want to marry him," I told Grandma. We both laughed. That ability—to laugh at the irony of a difficult decision—was another indication I made the right choice.

My heart's reaction to falling in love was to want to get married, but I gave my head time to think it through, and my head knew to wait.

Grandma married when she was twenty-one, but even though she married much sooner than most people do nowadays she learned a strange lesson in patience. You see, she and Grandpa had to keep their marriage secret for *ten years*! In those days, married women were often not allowed to work, and Grandma and Grandpa were a working-class couple who both needed jobs to make ends meet. During the Great Depression, and beyond, the few jobs available to women were often reserved for single women with no other means of support. Grandma worked at a five-and-dime store, and if her employer had found out she was married he would have fired her.

Grandma's situation was not uncommon; a few friends who worked with her were also married. They all knew about each other's husbands, but they relied on each other to keep a code of silence. At that time, losing a job meant you might not eat. Working-class people understood the importance of having friends in hard times, because they never knew when they might need each other. So they would never have compromised each other's employability by exposing each other. Sometimes people today forget the importance of that sort of honor code; now and then I've seen someone backstab a fellow employee for short-term gain. I think they're unwise, not just in terms of compassion, but also in terms of self-interest. When you stab someone in the back, you increase the chances they'll stab you when they can, and you decrease the number of people you can turn to when you need a helping hand. In short, you decrease the size of your support network. This harkens back to Grandma's advice, "Do not burn bridges."

Just to give you an idea of how critical to survival Grandma and Grandpa's secret was: they hid where they lived for the first ten years of their marriage, because that would have been a big giveaway. They lived together at her mother's house, as did many young couples. Another family member and her husband lived together in my great-grandmother's attic, and that was also very hush-hush. Such wives had to practice strict birth control or abstinence, because pregnancy would have cost them their jobs—right when they had another mouth to feed. That's one reason my mother wasn't born until 1941.

I believe that sharing such a huge sacrifice and secret, in service to the greater goals of a long-term partnership, strengthened my grandparents' relationship. This wasn't just a physical romance, friendship, or business arrangement. Their marriage was the deepest sort of loving commitment, in which two people worked as one toward a mutual goal. They waited to announce their marriage so they could ensure a better future, for themselves as individuals, for each other as partners, and for a future family they could only imagine. That kind of planning required their hearts to be in it, but they could never have made it through unless they had thought it through with their heads.

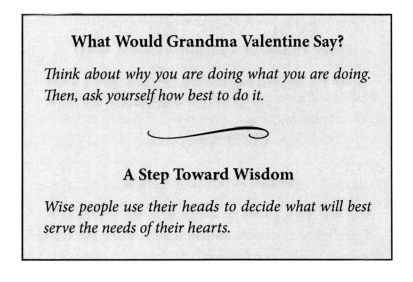

What Would Grandma Valentine Say?

Think about why you are doing what you are doing. Then, ask yourself how best to do it.

A Step Toward Wisdom

Wise people use their heads to decide what will best serve the needs of their hearts.

4

Who You Are,
Not What You Are

"In the end, people should be judged by their actions,
since in the end, it was actions that defined everyone."
– Nicholas Sparks

The Wisdom of Self-Reliance

Grandma and Grandpa Valentine were blue-collar workers. My grandpa didn't trust people who had a lot of money. His attitude wasn't vastly different from that of many people today who believe that if you're doing well financially, then you must be part of an evil conspiracy. That's not a new notion. It has just been repackaged and resold. My grandma was silent on the subject, as she was on any subject when she didn't agree with someone but knew that arguing wouldn't change that person's mind.

Grandma did not assume things about people based on their financial circumstances, the circumstances of their birth, or any of their external circumstances at all. She didn't assume that wealthy people were greedy and selfish, or that poor people were lazy and unmotivated. She felt that character was tied solely to an individual's actions, so she only held people accountable for their actions. If you did what you said you were going to do, and if you didn't sit around doing nothing while blaming other people for your lot in life—then you were okay by Grandma.

At the end of the day, Grandma's wisdom about people was simple: whatever their income, background, education, or social standing, people are no more or less than just people. No matter what you give a person or take away from a person, that person has a choice to either be honorable or not. If you want to be honorable, you will be, whatever your circumstances. That's what my grandma taught me.

If there was one thing Grandma admired most in anyone, it was self-reliance. The kind of self-reliance I'm talking about means much more than simply working to put food on the table, build a roof over your family's head, and send your kids to school. Grandma saw self-reliance as a strong internal foundation for living, something she called "spirit." I picture the kind of spirit Grandma talked about not as some vague ghostlike entity, but more like something solid with a backbone. Grandma fiercely defended the idea that each person is responsible for building up his or her own spirit. She firmly believed that spirit wasn't only what would bring someone through hard times, but that those hard times themselves were a powerful tool for strengthening the spirit.

"By sticking it out through tough times, people emerge from adversity with a stronger sense of efficacy."
– Albert Bandura

Psychologist Albert Bandura developed a well-known concept of self-efficacy: that is, a person's belief in his or her ability to deal with challenging encounters. Self-efficacy is different from self-esteem, which simply reflects how we feel about ourselves. Self-efficacy comes from actually facing and overcoming difficult challenges, which gives us the experience to know that we can overcome challenges in the future. The more we find out what we can do, the more we believe we can do; the more we believe we can do, the more we invest in our goals; and the more we invest in our goals, the greater the likelihood that we'll accomplish them.

It turns out that people with low self-efficacy experience a lot of anxiety, hopelessness, and anger. They find it harder to bounce back after adversity. Meanwhile, those with high self-efficacy experience more fulfillment, calmness, and decisiveness. They're self-motivated and resilient after setbacks. Research has shown that belief in one's ability to cope is a stronger predictor of success than objectively possessing the knowledge necessary to get a task done.

Society encourages self-efficacy in young people when it teaches them that success is not primarily a result of talent— over which they have little control—but rather comes from learning the necessary tasks to achieve a goal, and then doing them until one becomes good at them. As Malcolm Gladwell cites in *Outliers*, there is a "10,000-Hour Rule" that applies to most pursuits in life. Gladwell asserts that it takes about 10,000 hours of practice to become an expert at something. If you work at something long enough, you receive the rewarding feeling of self-efficacy, which encourages you to continue until you attain that magical 10,000 hours when success is within reach. Researchers at multiple universities have discovered that self-efficacy is a greater predictor of success in life than natural talent or intellect.

Helping Others Help Themselves

As great debaters regarding many aspects of the U.S. government, Grandma and I spent much time discussing the poor performance of many well-intended government welfare programs, starting with President Franklin D. Roosevelt's New Deal and extending through current times. Her greatest criticism of such programs was the effect they had on breaking the human spirit. I could as easily say that she thought it was breaking people's sense of self-efficacy.

Grandma was all for charitable assistance for the less fortunate, and all for lending her neighbor a helping hand, whether through private or public programs. Her problem with welfare was that it typically had no effective mechanism to encourage people to return to self-sufficiency so they could earn greater rewards and, through that, feel good about themselves and build their spirit back up.

In 1996, Grandma and I were both excited when President Bill Clinton signed into law the Personal Responsibility and Work Opportunity Reconciliation Act, his version of welfare-to-work. The plan succeeded in helping people in times of need while also encouraging them to take specific steps to get back to work. Today only one welfare program resulting from that 1996 law continues to specifically promote self-reliance: Temporary Assistance for Needy Families, or TANF, which has moved 2.8 million families off welfare rolls and into jobs. But even though TANF has been successful, there are few if any other federal welfare programs that have undergone similar reforms.

I agree with Grandma, that we help people most when we effectively give them the tools they need to find work, which helps them build a sense of self-reliance and, consequently, self-efficacy, that will serve them long term. Instead, in most states today, many welfare programs pay more than a minimum-wage job, which doesn't provide people much incentive to learn to do things on their own. So they're discouraged from engaging in the skill development that leads to self-efficacy.

My grandma learned first-hand what it was like to help poor people through a crisis. Those people were her relatives. Her sister's husband was a factory worker who was tragically killed on the job in the 1940s. His wife and two infant daughters received no compensation for their tremendous loss. Grandma and Grandpa decide to help support them so they would not go hungry or homeless. They did that because they believed family helps family, one of the first lessons they had learned as immigrants. Grandma and Grandpa believed it was important for her sister to have the option to stay at home to raise her children, so they helped them for several years.

Grandma's sister later signed up for New Deal benefits, and she used that support system for years without any incentive to ever stop. I never brought up the subject of how this impacted my great-aunt's spirit, or that of her children, because I knew that Grandma was very fond of her sister. I didn't want to risk upsetting her, but I knew Grandma well enough to feel her concern for her sister's well being.

Thanks to Grandma sharing her family's experiences with me, I've grown into someone who is always happy to give people a hand *up* but who shies away from giving a handout. Not because I don't want to help, but because I want to give people meaningful help. I've found that one of life's greatest gifts is to help other people discover how to stand on their own two feet.

Living in downtown Chicago for many years helped reinforce that perspective for me. When I lived in Chicago, I walked to work daily. My apartment was just over a mile from my office, and sitting at a desk job all day made me eager for physical activity, so I enjoyed getting to work on foot. On my way to work, I passed people who frantically approached others with the same story day after day: "I was robbed last night and need money for a bus ticket home." Each time I heard those con artists, I shook my head, hoping their marks would not be taken in.

I saw the same panhandlers for weeks on end. Sometimes they would go away for a while, but they'd be back in a few months. I knew that some people gave them money, and the fact that the panhandlers kept returning made it clear that they had no jobs. That experience taught me that giving people cash without attaching it to skill, effort, or positive behavior was not a real help to them. It only left them on the street without so much as their honor. It seems to me that this sort of "help," well intentioned as it may be, is almost worse than no help at all.

Beyond The Circumstances of Our Birth

My Grandpa Valentine was abandoned in America by his parents, who left to return to Europe. The details of his childhood are unclear to me because he refused to talk about it to anyone but Grandma, who did not share much either.

My family and I believe that this shared confidence was one of the bonds they had that strengthened their closeness. What I know about Grandpa Valentine's youth is this:

When Jimmy (Grandpa Valentine) was small his mother abandoned him to return to France and was never heard from again. His father then abandoned him to the care of an aunt who stayed in America. Jimmy and his father had little contact throughout his childhood. So when his father returned to England, Jimmy did not trust him enough to go with him. Grandpa Valentine never spoke to his parents again for the rest of their lives.

Even after my grandpa passed away, my grandma never said a word about his childhood. However she did tell me that orphans during Grandpa's time, and long before that, were considered innately flawed. In the eyes of the world, when a child had parents who had either died or abandoned them, it reflected poorly on that child. If you were an orphan or abandoned, many people believed that either God had punished you for a reason, or you came from defective family stock, or you came from bad parents and would therefore become bad like them. Society felt justified in rejecting such children. It was as if everyone who admitted to being an orphan had a red "O" embroidered on their clothes ever after.

My grandma never had those kinds of thoughts about orphaned or abandoned children. She reserved judgment until she got to know someone, rather than letting other people's judgments sway her. When mutual friends introduced her to my grandpa, she decided for herself that he was a good guy, regardless of people's preconceived notions about his sad upbringing. To the joy of their friends, their romance blossomed quickly into unconditional trust and acceptance that would last a lifetime. She felt a profound, soulful connection with my grandfather, and she trusted her feelings and her judgment enough to marry him. Her vindication was sixty-six years of happy, loving marriage.

"Never judge people based on their circumstances or their past. Judge them for who they are, not what they are."
— Grandma Valentine

Grandma thought judging someone based on the circumstances of his birth, or any circumstances other than his observable actions, was silly. If a child was rejected by his parents it could never be the child's fault. Children are not responsible for their parents' behavior. Even if a child misbehaved, only a terrible parent would abandon him. How can we assign lack of character to a child, someone who has not had a chance to develop?

If you don't think people engage in that sort of pre-judgment today, think about foster kids or street kids. Those are today's orphans, and many people treat them just as much like pariahs as ever, believing that their circumstances are the results of their actions, or that their families are so messed up that the children are beyond saving. Even though there are some children who have truly lost their families, there are many other children in the system who have not been orphaned and have had breakdowns in their families for other reasons. So onlookers sometimes draw dark conclusions about how the children came to be part of the foster care system or to live on the streets.

Today's kids are often judged based on their ability to buy the "right" clothing, have the "right" friends, play on the "right" sports team, or basically display a desirable situation that implies power in America: youth, looks, and money. Those things are typically not in a child's control, but are instead a result of the parents' capabilities, circumstances, and choices. Yet such judgments are widely held attitudes cast by people of all ages. Grandma only wanted to know three things about young people before she would give them a chance: do they work hard, are they honest, and do they have a can-do attitude?

Grandma had deep empathy, an important quality to possess if you want to attain true wisdom. She understood that our actions and our luck both play a role in the quality of our lives. She also understood where luck and circumstances beyond our control leave off, and where attitude and hard work begin. Bad luck gave Grandpa his childhood circumstances. His parents returned to Europe, leaving him to largely fend for himself, although he relied on some support from his kind aunt. But he didn't let his absent parents take his spirit with them. His positive attitude made him a dreamer, and his belief in hard work made him a successful provider. That was all Grandma needed to know. She understood how much it hurt him when his parents left him, as if he had done something wrong. I believe that the rejection he had overcome only made her more devoted to him.

No doubt some of Grandma's empathy came from personal experience. If empathy is the ability to understand and share the feelings of another, that cannot happen unless we've first felt similar feelings ourselves. As German immigrants in Chicago in the 1890s, her family had not been high on the class scale. People made certain assumptions about immigrants in general, not just Germans, before they had the opportunity to say or do anything wrong. So Grandma knew what it was like not to be valued for *who* she was, but only to be disregarded for what she was.

"The most beautiful people we have known are those who have known defeat, known suffering, known struggle, known loss, and have found their way out of the depths. These persons have an appreciation, a sensitivity, and an understanding of life that fills them with compassion, gentleness, and a deep loving concern."
— Elisabeth Kübler-Ross

Grandma taught me to look at only two things in making any judgments about people: 1) How does that person act? 2) How does that person treat other people?

Grandpa could be a little bit more limited than Grandma in his views, tending to make negative judgments about people just because they were wealthy. Still, he had a big heart for most people, especially working-class people like himself. Grandpa worked a lot of different blue-collar jobs, usually in restaurants. He worked as a maître d' at the M&M Club in Chicago, an exclusive club that attracted high-powered wealthy and political types back in the 1930s, '40s and '50s, including Joseph Kennedy, patriarch of the Kennedy clan. Grandpa once met Joe Kennedy while on the job at the M&M Club. Although Grandpa was a Democrat, it only took that one meeting for him to take an instant dislike to the man. He did not care for Kennedy's poor treatment of the servers and other club personnel. He said Kennedy was "mean and condescending to everyone around him." On that scale of judgment, Grandma and Grandpa agreed. They didn't judge a powerful man by how much other powerful people liked him, but by how he treated those less powerful than himself.

Mr. Kennedy signed a dollar bill for Grandpa as a tip, and Grandpa saved it, but he made sure we knew, "I don't value it. I just thought someday it might be worth something. So I saved it in case it might help my own children someday." The family's well-being was more important than personal opinion. Family always came first.

Making A Career of Wisdom

Relationships were at the root of Grandma's wisdom and understanding of the world. Although she did not have formal education, she had a deep understanding of human motivations. Grandma often asserted that human nature had not changed over time. Humans were mostly predictable, which made it easier for her to take the correct course of action based on experience. Although she used old-fashioned phrasing at times, I recognized that her wisdom had practical applications that crossed generations. Most of our conversations were grounded in basic psychology, even when she didn't know the modern vocabulary for it, so I trusted her wisdom to help me keep my problems with other people in perspective.

The most important time in my life that Grandma helped me navigate was my first journey into the corporate world, right out of college. My first corporate position was at a large company where I immediately witnessed the stereotypical atmosphere of colleagues vying for control and status. It only took adding one mean-spirited, maniacal mid-level manager to an otherwise pleasant professional experience to make it a miserable environment.

I witnessed that manager picking on the weak and back-stabbing the strong, until I questioned whether maintaining surface calm and not giving in to my emotions was really the way to go. Behaving in a calm and sensible manner wasn't changing the situation. I thought it only moral to defend those in his path who were unable to stand up for themselves. But when I did stand up for others, it did little to help the situation. Instead, it increased the suffering of those I defended and moved me up his list of priority targets.

Even in my twenties, I understood that anyone interested in self-preservation would seek wise counsel before embarking on an extreme course of action. So as usual, I called Grandma. She carefully listened and questioned me about all aspects of the situation and the people involved, not in one sitting but over several conversations, which kept me from hasty action. She told me about similar mistreatment of employees that she had witnessed at her job in the 1930s, a time when employers had more control and employees had fewer rights than today. Workers were deemed so readily replaceable that even a gossipy whisper about someone engaged in wrongdoing could result in that person's immediate dismissal.

Grandma suggested that, although I had correctly judged my supervisor as a difficult and unprofessional manager bent on building his success by tearing others down, sacrificing myself would do nobody any good. I had judged him for who he was—a bad guy—not what he was—my boss—but that hadn't improved my results. Even though I knew who I was—a dependable, professional employee and a caring person—upper management only knew what I was—a low-level employee. Grandma's main advice was "do not burn bridges." She instead suggested that I use my positive disposition and strength to persevere until I could find new employment. Grandma believed that if I delivered my best consistently, without engaging in confrontation, it would demonstrate good character—which might be appreciated by the higher executives over time. So far, the higher ups had not been party to any of the underhanded shenanigans of my supervisor, so those were relationships that might well be worth maintaining.

In times of great stress or adversity, it's always best to keep busy, to plow your anger and your energy into something positive.
— Lee Iacocca

Grandma was not suggesting I roll over and never speak up at all. I did let the manager know when I disagreed with him, but only in the most civil, limited terms, and only when to do otherwise would compromise my integrity. As he fought for more control through undignified and unethical methods, my stress was likely apparent to others. But Grandma taught me to keep things in perspective, to remember that this was just my first job out of college, in a promising career, and that it wouldn't do for me to ruin my future over one bad apple. For the moment, my supervisor had the ear of upper management and was happy to smear my reputation with negative commentary. There wasn't much opportunity to clear my name without looking whiny and defensive.

Grandma had explained to me that advancing one's own agenda by stepping on others was a tactic used by gangsters. But she was more concerned that I not do anything to jeopardize my spirit and self-worth, rather than whether or not I might lose my job. "Remember, Gabrielle, an industrious person will never be down for long. You can always find employment again, because you're the type of person who is always willing to educate yourself and work hard."

I did what Grandma advised. I continued to make a positive contribution while building up a work history and keeping my eyes open for better opportunities. My wait was rewarded.

One day, I happened to have a conversation about a new project with someone in upper management. Instead of using that time to complain or plea for rescue, which might have put a negative spin on the interaction, I did the something else Grandma had suggested: I asked the executive for his advice. In other words, I made it clear that I respected his ability and authority, and I put him in the driver's seat of the conversation. I told him that I was capable of doing the heavy lifting on the new project, but that I could use some additional perspective from him since I was not privy to many management discussions. The executive I spoke to did more than offer advice; he confirmed that he knew about the antics of the middle manager and that he saw through the man's negative discourse. He suggested that the only solution to help me perform at my best was to get me out from under that supervisor. He didn't just talk about it. Because I'd shown initiative, he supported me by privately facilitating my transfer to another department.

During that entire time, as I tried to figure out how to move my career forward while under the thumb of a poor manager, Grandma stuck by my side with guidance. Her key phrase was always, "Keep things in perspective." She knew that if I committed to working hard with integrity, then that experience would be little more than a brief teachable moment in a long, fruitful career. She was right. I sidestepped the power struggle and had an enjoyable career in that company for nearly ten years. I appreciated what that situation taught me about using strategy in a corporate setting, a lesson that has translated to other environments with similar structures and players.

The greatest lesson Grandma and I discussed was how power corrupts if you don't recognize the temptations that come with it. She believed that, if we're not vigilant, the pursuit of power can destroy our perspective. She said that only the strongest people can resist the corrupting influence of increasing power. In her opinion, keeping that firmly in mind would help me sort out the kind of high-quality people I wanted to align myself with. She forgave people who made bad decisions because power corrupted them. She knew they weren't necessarily bad people, just weak. Still, good or bad, they were not the people I would be wise to rely on in the future.

I would come to learn that even good people can make bad decisions. But my purpose in life was not to worry about whether or not other people were good or bad. My purpose was to work on being the best of myself and making the right decisions for me.

"Knowing others is intelligence; knowing yourself is true wisdom. Mastering others is strength; mastering yourself is true power."
– Lao Tzu, Tao Te Ching

We're More than Our Pasts

Shortly after my fiancé Dylan and I got engaged, I took him to meet Grandma. He knew how special she was to me and he took meeting her as an honor. Meanwhile, she had heard much about him during our whirlwind romance. Although Dylan and I had met in business school years before, we had only dated for eight months prior to getting engaged. Meeting the parents is a matter of course in a serious relationship, but this was something more. He instantly knew that my grandma's opinion was one I deeply valued.

When they met, Grandma picked up right away on two of Dylan's best qualities: humility and sincerity. His was not false humility, but a truly humble nature tempered with self-respect. From that place, he was able to treat her with respect and warmth. It was clearly important to him to make a good impression on her, but he didn't put on any phony manners to achieve that.

We sat with Grandma in her living room and spoke about each other and our relationship. The fast pace of our romance and engagement prompted a lot of questions. I had kept Grandma updated on the phone, and I realized she wasn't fishing for new information on our relationship so much as giving herself a chance to observe how Dylan responded, how he carried himself, and how he treated me. Did he show me respect during the conversation? What was the tone of his answers? What could his outlook on a variety of topics reveal about his values? She was a detective and she was politely investigating him. Luckily for me, Dylan was himself—his best self. When he briefly left the room to go next door and say hello to my Aunt June and Uncle Jim, Grandma confided in me, "Ahhh, I like him. He'll be good for you. He's a nice man."

I had instinctively known that Grandma would like him, because I had adopted her yardstick for measuring people's worth: based on their actions, not their circumstances, their past, or their charm. I put a lot of stock in Grandma's assessments of people and was confident our judgment would coincide. I'm glad she had a chance to meet Dylan and to weigh in with her wisdom on the most important choice of my life. A few months later she passed away. It meant a lot to me to know she had confidence that I would continue in the right direction after she was gone. She and I were right: Dylan and I have had a wonderful marriage for thirteen years.

What Would Grandma Valentine Say?

Do not judge character by what people say, but by what they do.

A Step Toward Wisdom

We are not the pasts we come from, over which we have no control. We are the people we decide to be in the present, by the actions we choose today.

5

Wisdom is Neither Prejudiced Nor Politically Correct

"Man is always inclined to be intolerant towards the thing, or person, he hasn't taken the time adequately to understand..."
– Robert R. Brown, Episcopal Bishop

Bias Opposes or Favors Others Without Reason

When Martin Luther King, Jr. said, "I have a dream that my four little children will one day live in a nation where they will not be judged by the color of their skin but by the content of their character," my Grandma was impressed with his wisdom. It was a new iteration of what she had long believed: that people should be judged based on *who* they are, not *what* they are. However, she did not have the opportunity for a lot of personal experiences with African Americans during her era in Chicago.

For many years, Grandma lived in a working-class neighborhood of European immigrants. When black neighbors first moved into the neighborhood, she accepted them on a case-by-case basis, as she would anyone. She was friendly to the new neighbors she came in contact with, and many of them were equally friendly to her. Not everyone in the neighborhood was as tolerant as Grandma, whether newcomers or old-timers. As the income level of the neighborhood went down, so did the tolerance level. Many blacks feared whites, and many whites feared blacks. Racial tensions grew, and crime rose.

Grandma and Grandpa felt forced to flee the situation in the early 1980s. Grandma struggled with the thought that violence and discord had forced her to flee her neighborhood for a safer place to live. I knew from my conversations with her that she still believed in Dr. King's dream and the words he offered to express his expectations of people of any color or creed. However, many neighbors who had lived through those times with her responded in a more generalized way, developing more jaded feelings. Although Grandma did not agree with unsavory comments about who people were, she did not waste her breath trying to change their minds. If she had personally witnessed anyone being abused or treated unfairly, she would have found it worthwhile to defend that individual. But Grandma simply didn't believe in wasting time and energy in trying to impose her thoughts and feelings on others.

"People are going to think what they want to think until they're ready to think different."
— Grandma Valentine

Grandma's philosophy was to observe and learn, not necessarily to insert herself into situations. She allowed people to exist as they were, even when she felt sure they were wrong. If there was no benefit to speaking, then silence was better.

My Aunt June, who lived in the same condominium building as my grandparents, sometimes said something like, and I paraphrase, "It's terrible. We should not have been forced to move. The neighborhood is dangerous now. The people in it don't care, they don't get along, and I'm tired of it."

Grandma would reply, "Yes, June…Yes, June…Yes June," with an exaggerated patience that let anyone who was paying attention understand that she was not in complete agreement. Rather than engage in a confrontation that was sure to go nowhere, she took the path of diplomacy, and hinted that she would prefer a change of subject.

Many Americans have lived through experiences similar to my family's story on the North Side of Chicago. Whether someone is of a different ethnicity, religion, race, or sexual orientation, it seems to create strife among various populations struggling to understand the implications of including different people in their community. Diversity has always challenged America, which is why striving to find shared values and beliefs, religious or not, is important to developing a community. When people don't make that effort, extreme behavior can result. For example, some groups seek to impose their religious beliefs on others, to the point of threatening to expunge or kill those who don't convert. Mistrust of people from other cultures and races is nothing new. If you traveled back centuries in time, you would find Muslims and Christians fighting in North Africa, Spain, and the Middle East. Ancestral memories of discrimination, expulsion, and war get passed down for generations and can cause centuries of ill will.

When Grandma and I talked, she clued me into her thinking. She knew that the discipline to analyze the situation in her North Side Chicago neighborhood involved layers of issues and a variety of individuals—most of whom were *not* criminals. She also knew that not everyone possessed this discipline and ability. She realized that many people on both sides of the issue found it easier to stack up evidence that the opposing side was the guiltier party. This is a common reaction when people try to convince third parties to advocate for their side. Grandma knew that this gave many people in the situation a false sense of vindication.

In Grandma's opinion, it was better to leave the neighborhood that she loved because healing the divide would require intensive work, mutual respect, and compromise from all sides. It was a tough goal that she believed many in the situation were not brave enough to achieve.

The Neocortex versus The Amygdala

In my experience, people's ability to accept differences in others has steadily decreased in my lifetime, while a militant approach of a few telling the many how to think, act, and make decisions has increased. This command and control approach is not new or original but has occurred over and over throughout human history. It just contracts and expands in different cultures, societies, and communities over time.

The Great American Experiment as set forth in our Declaration of Independence, Bill of Rights, and U.S. Constitution and discussed in the Federalist Papers, showed how a set of highly defined freedoms can bring out tremendous spirit and ambition in the human race. However, our freedoms in the United States come with challenges that need to be carefully understood. The freedom to express an opinion, right or wrong, has been in danger over the course of human history. For those who hold power over large populations, freedom to express opinions poses a danger to their own power. Thus, we have the birth of political correctness as a desired trait. Yet, freedom to express opinions, thoughts, and ideas is a key component of developing wisdom.

Wisdom requires exchanging ideas and listening to others. How can we grow mentally and emotionally if societal pressure, in other words political correctness, does not allow us to explore conversations with open and inquisitive minds?

Why is the freedom to express our opinions so important, even when they might offend others? Let's go back to the North Side of Chicago. Scientific research tells us that the common neighborhood reaction of stereotyping and my grandma's reaction of withholding judgment are both survival responses, but each involves different parts of the brain.

Recent research in social neuroscience has revealed that prejudiced reactions are linked to rapidly activated structures in the brain, such as the amygdala, which is associated with reactions of fear, disgust, and distrust. The amygdala likely developed long ago in human evolution, and it contains simple mechanisms for detecting "us" versus "them," and for automatically treating "them" as a threat. That may be a helpful survival response in a tribal or nomadic society where groups are widely separated, territorial, and potentially violent. However, that sort of prejudice is contrary to survival and growth in a modern civilized society, where cooperation and unity are important.

Neuroscientists have discovered that, during evolution, the human brain didn't simply get larger. It also developed new structures, such as the neocortex, or outer layer of our brain, which grew atop the older subcortex, or what some people call our "lizard" brain. The subcortex is wired for faster responses, which makes it great for responding to sudden threats or changes. The neocortex is wired to fine-tune and augment the functions of the subcortex. So it may be that all of us have an instantaneous subcortical response of fear or anger toward people our senses identify as being of a different "tribe." What makes some people less prejudiced and more egalitarian is that they more effectively engage their neocortex to ignore differences in favor of higher goals, whether they're asking a stranger for directions, evaluating an employee, or making a new friend.

A few years ago, New York University psychologist David Amodio and his colleagues conducted a series of experiments in which they studied the neural mechanisms that enable people to control their behavior in the face of automatic prejudices. In one study, the electrical activity in people's brains was studied via EEG (electroencephalogram) during a computer task in which they looked at faces and then identified various objects as either guns or tools. Just before each gun or tool appeared, the face of either a white or a black person flashed briefly on the screen. Some participants reacted to the stereotype of African Americans as dangerous and tended to see more guns after seeing a black face, which made them give more incorrect answers. Here comes the interesting part: according to their EEG, those people who were less likely to correlate black faces with weapons also showed greater activity in their left prefrontal cortex, a region associated with greater self-control. In other words, the less prejudiced subjects did not rely on automatic responses prompted by the subcortex, but on more controlled thought.

Perhaps one of the biggest surprises from that test is this: the frontal cortical activity of the people who showed *less* prejudice also seemed to tune other regions of the brain to take *more* notice of the difference between black and white faces. When they cued themselves to pay *more* attention to race, they were better able to adjust their behavior to respond with *less* prejudice. Those subjects were more accurate in identifying tools versus weapons. One conclusion is that people who tend to be less prejudiced, are those who make conscious note of differences and then choose to focus on a goal without regard to those differences.

The above NYU study indicates that we humans can train ourselves to override our prejudices involving races different from ourselves. And if we achieve more goals as a result, we're more likely in future to respond positively to people who appear different.

In another study, by NYU social psychologist Jay van Bavel, participants were told they would be playing a game, and they were shown photos of black people and white people. They were told that specific people in the photos would be on their team, while others would be on the opposing team. Van Bavel scanned participants' brains while they looked at the faces. It turns out that their amygdalas were more active while they viewed faces of the opposing team, regardless of race. This implies that we might be able to reduce our amygdala's automatic prejudicial responses just by convincing people they're all on the same team, whether that's a team of coworkers, neighbors, or fellow citizens.

Wisdom Makes No Assumptions

Although Grandma taught me the value of making deductions about a situation without knowing every last detail, she also taught me the value of withholding judgments about someone until I learn as many details as possible through interacting with that person. It's easiest to see this lesson in terms of bias based on race, culture, religion, politics, and such. But even that sort of list can narrow the lesson. The idea was that each and every person is a blank slate until I've had time to get to know how that person behaves and whether that behavior reflects values I can respect.

To allow each person the opportunity of being a blank slate is a gift to him and to me. It allows each of us the opportunity to leave our past experiences at the door and invent our best possible selves anew. Did you ever go to a new school or new job and think, "Ah, a fresh start! These people know little about me, so I'm free to become a new me!" Those who make assumptions can spoil that opportunity.

Imagine the space we create for others when we give them the gift of letting them paint a new picture of themselves for us, brimming with positive possibilities. To do that, we need to do our best to let go of our prejudices around gender, age, race, sexual orientation, religion, politics, and so on. To create the best opportunity for a positive and mutually beneficial relationship, we also need to let go of many other things we think we know about other people.

Let's start by admitting that some of our stereotypes can sometimes prove correct: someone who walks around with a sour look on his face daily might be a negative person, someone who slouches at her desk all the time might be apathetic, and someone who fidgets a lot at meetings might have anxiety issues. Knowing that some people make judgments like these on first meeting is a good reminder to stay on top of our behavioral quirks. However, when we look at others we can't always size these things up accurately in just one or two meetings, and we risk missing out on opportunities when we dismiss people based on snap impressions that don't reveal their deep-down values. It is the core values underneath those exterior impressions that can make someone a valuable addition to our life and experience.

My grandma taught me not only to consider what I know about a person, but what I cannot know. For example: you might meet someone who seems to be smiling too hard, so the temptation is to assume that person's a phony, but maybe he's shy, or maybe he's nervous meeting new people. You might meet someone who acts distracted, so the temptation is to assume she's an airhead, when maybe her dog just died. Maybe you meet a guy who speaks loudly and you think he's pompous, when maybe he simply has a hearing problem.

It takes time to learn a person, and it's hard to know how much time it takes. Me? I take as much time as the situation permits. Sure, sometimes I realize early on that a person is going to be difficult for me to work with or spend time with, so if there's a way to gracefully exit the relationship while getting both our needs met, then I'll choose that route. Otherwise, if I'm stuck with someone I'm tempted to judge, I find I get better results when I take the time to look for the best I can find in the person and focus on that.

"I look only to the good qualities of men. Not being faultless myself, I won't presume to probe into the faults of others."
— Mahatma Gandhi

Dealing with People Who Are Different

Grandma and Grandpa owned their hot dog and hamburger restaurant into their retirement years, and didn't sell it until the mid-seventies. After they sold it they had less contact with the working world, but Grandma still hung onto her value of only judging people by their actions. When I entered the working world and began to bring my workplace issues to Grandma, those issues typically involved personality differences with coworkers or conflicts over office politics. Whenever I explained a problem I was having with a colleague, she never asked the color, religion, or political party of the person I was talking about. She didn't believe she needed to know that information to initially analyze the situation. Because she never asked those questions, it told me that sort of information wasn't important. That's not to say I might not have come to that conclusion on my own, but rather to credit Grandma for all the years she modeled discipline in analyzing people based only on their relevant choices and actions.

Wisdom is always a work in progress, and, like anyone, sometimes I'm tempted to make assumptions about other people. That's normal as the human brain tries to categorize things and seek patterns: Is this item edible? Is this situation life-threatening? Is this person a potential business partner? Is this person part of my tribe, or a threat to my tribe and me?

To be accepting of people who are different, especially those with different cultural values, sometimes requires me to recognize my preconceived notions and suppress them.

In the early 1990s, I volunteered with the Youth Motivation Program, or "YPM," in Chicago. My responsibilities included visiting public high schools in the city and speaking with students to inspire them. I had developed a repertoire of talking points so I could tailor my subject matter to the schools I visited, depending on their neighborhoods and challenges. One high school I visited was more than half Hispanic, at least one-third African American, and the remaining fraction a mix of different ethnicities. The school faced many challenges due to drug use, difficult family situations, and youth crime.

As I walked the stairways with my student guides, passing security guards at key points, I knew that the presentation I had decided to use on the power of dreaming would be a good one. My talk focused on people from a variety of environments who followed their dreams and the steps they took to make their dreams a reality. I had already learned that kids didn't want to only hear success stories, they also wanted to know how to do things for themselves. They needed examples of blueprints they could follow on their own since most of them did not have home support or resources to help them. Since I was still in my early twenties, I worked hard to keep the presentation punchy and hip so they would feel engaged.

I entered a full classroom and instantly saw that the thirty-five faces displayed a wide variety of interest levels, from "I'd rather be anywhere but here" to "I wonder what she has to say?" Even though I was talking to high school students, I always dressed as if I were going to the office: business suit, pearls, nicely styled hair, and makeup. I believed, and still do, that the details are important. Young people need to know that the way they present themselves matters.

After I gave them a brief overview of who I was and what I did, I launched into my presentation on having and achieving dreams. A couple of girls in front lit up at certain points. Others pretended not to listen, but I could tell I had their attention too when I shifted to points they connected with. Face it: even kids who have given up know what it means to dream. The class seemed to enjoy it, or at least not heckle it, except for one young man at the back.

My challenger was around fifteen with an intense stare. When I took questions, he stood to ask his. He had a confrontational stance, so I responded by leaning back against the teacher's desk, keeping my posture welcoming and open. He then entered into a litany of aggressive questions and comments in a tone that suggested he represented the class. I sensed from his confidence, and their attentiveness, that he did represent many of them to a certain extent, which gave me pause. I made sure to completely hear him out before I responded so that I could reach out to the entire room with a caring response.

He asked, "Why should we listen to you? You're not like us. You don't know our life. This is bunk. I don't need to listen to this crap. Who are you anyway?" He went on in this vein for a couple of minutes. Then he stopped, still standing, waiting.

His challenging stance seemed to pose a host of questions: What is she going to do? Is she scared, offended, angry? Will she stomp out of the room and give up on everyone in the class as a lost cause? I resisted the temptation to stereotype his response as an ignorant attack, and instead applied empathy, trying to see things from his viewpoint. That moment of wisdom told me that he was not trying to attack me, but to protect himself and the group. So I did not treat it as an attack.

Instead I slowly and confidently rose from the edge of the desk and said something to this effect, "Thank you for your thoughts. I can understand how you think I can't possibly understand your situation. But I do. You don't know my complete past or what I've done to get to where I am. I don't wear my problems and feelings on my sleeve, so it must be tough to see how I'm like you. But I don't want to argue about me being here and you liking it or not. I'm here because all of you need to learn how to dream about the potential all of you have. I want to give all of you ideas on how you can get yourself ahead and create a cool future for yourselves. When the Youth Motivation Program called me, they gave me a couple of choices on which school I could visit. I had my choice of schools that were easy and safe, and a couple of schools, like yours, that were more dangerous for me personally. I chose yours because I thought there was potential here that I could inspire. This was the school with the most problems, but that doesn't mean all of you don't have great possibilities for your futures. The woman coordinating this visit thanked me over and over because she said this would be a tough speaking spot to fill."

At that point, I paused and looked around to make sure all of the kids were looking at me. I wanted them to recognize that the chaos in their school was mostly of their own doing and that their behavior had consequences, such as the scary reputation they had created.

Softly but firmly, I ended with, "I came because I was the one who cared enough to come."

He sat down, his demeanor softened but still angry. I suppose some of it might have been the rebellious teenager in him. But he didn't say anything else. A couple of the students shared friendly, apologetic smiles with me. No one else raised their hands. The entire class had a lot to think about. Moments later the class bell rang and the kids rushed to the exits. I gathered my materials to leave.

The teacher walked over and said, "They're a tough group, but good kids. I appreciate what you said. I think they heard and it all helps. And I am sorry about Juan. He's angry."

"I'm glad he said something," I said. "I want him to know that he has a voice and that it's good to question how things are relevant to their world. Hopefully, knowing there are people who are strangers who care will make a difference to a few of them. Thank you for letting me visit. Good luck." I walked out to my student guides who escorted me off the premises.

Some Differences Aren't Obvious

Preconceived notions are not necessarily tied to skin color, ethnic features, accents, or clothing. It could be a tone of voice that reminds me of someone who picked on me in elementary school, or some other mistaken association based on the situation or surroundings. Maybe I meet someone who's standing in the break room pouring hot water to make cocoa, and maybe it reminds me of the time my mother poured me a cup of cocoa when I was five and I burned my tongue. So I have a visceral reaction to the person pouring hot water now based on my bad experience with hot water in the past. I might not be aware of the association at first, but wisdom asks me to pause for a moment and ask myself what's really bothering me.

Once I identify the problem, wisdom says, "Stop! Don't generalize! I'm sorry you burned your tongue when you were five, but let's look at this new lady holding this new cup of hot water. What is she doing with it?"

"Well, she's just drinking it."

"And is that hurting you?"

"No."

"So do you think you can recognize that this may not be the same situation as before and withhold judgment until this woman gives you reason to think she'll burn you?"

Because I hold Grandma's wisdom, I answer, "Yes."

Actually, that's the way I approach people in general, because I'm focused on achieving my goals regardless of the differences I see around me. My primary goal: to share a deep love of people and a desire to contribute to the world. Because of my goal, I prefer to assume people have good intentions until they clearly reveal otherwise.

It takes some pretty active ill will for someone to harm me. Usually negative people give clear signs that they're going to be negative. I read those signs and respect them; in other words, I give a wide berth to people who seem to poison the social atmosphere. Otherwise, everyone gets the benefit of the doubt, until and unless they do something that makes it clear they don't deserve it anymore. Even then, I give people a chance to prove they did harm by accident and are willing to make amends so we can move on toward positive mutual goals in future.

Although racial and religious prejudices are the ones we hear about most, I would suggest that every day we encounter within ourselves simple, personal preconceived notions. The only way to get past those is to first admit that we all have them. Then truly wise people set those aside, because preconceived notions set unnecessary boundaries that can limit us. Unnecessary boundaries can inhibit the ability to learn new ideas and to work with others to create new things.

The ability to set aside preconceived notions is critical to success at any aspect of life. While it can be beneficial to learn from past mistakes, or to recognize the danger in new situations based on dangers you faced in the past, it's just too limiting to allow all of your past experiences with other people to shape your experience of a new person. Yes, experience is important, but we must never forget that the most important question is what is happening right now, in the moment, in *this* reality? If I introduce all of my old baggage into a situation with a new person, what I see might look far different from reality.

It's not easy to set aside our old baggage, and those heavy reminders from the past may make us uncomfortable and even frightened in new situations. But if we want to give ourselves the opportunity to let in new people with whom we can learn and grow and contribute, then we must be willing to go through the discomfort and fear. Because on the other side is the joy of discovering that people will not always let us down, that in fact they may contribute to us in ways we never imagined.

What Would Grandma Valentine Say?

Things aren't always what they appear. Use your head and every sense you can muster. Gather your own information and use it. Be careful not to assume.

A Step Toward Wisdom

If we remain objective, even as the pull of subjectivity tempts us, we open the door to new possibilities, and people who are different will be part of those possibilities.

6

Wisdom Does Not Burn Bridges

"When one burns one's bridges, what a very nice fire it makes."
– Dylan Thomas

You Don't Have to Like Everyone

Grandma always walked the tightrope of respect and honesty. She was frank with her daughters, and her main piece of advice for all of us was, "Don't burn bridges." She didn't believe it was ever necessary to do that. She believed a wise person who practiced patience and thoughtfulness could always find a way around, over, or through any conflict, without having to blow up a relationship or tear down another person. She always told me, "You do not have to like people to get along with them."

"If you have to associate with difficult people, take emotion out of the conversation. Don't fall for attempts to put emotion into the conversation, especially if it's meant to insult anyone."
– Grandma Valentine

Her advice was to take negative emotion out of the equation whenever it threatened to unsettle my internal harmony—what I've since learned to call my homeostasis. She made it clear that it wasn't just my own negative emotions I should sublimate, but also those of difficult people who wanted to bring negativity to the table. The idea wasn't to judge them, but to simply not engage with them when they took a position meant to tear me down or tear others down. Grandma's advice in that arena was most useful to me in my business career, where my goals often required me to maintain relationships with difficult people.

Burned Bridges

8I have made the mistake of burning a few bridges in my lifetime, but have learned something from these experiences each time. Early in my career, I worked for a company that hired me to assist with the workload of one of its full-time employees, an administrative assistant. This colleague had held her position for several years and she made it clear she was proud of running a tight ship. No one made mistakes in her area, not the employees, not her colleagues, and not the customers.

She was assigned to train me, and at first I was excited to work with her. I appreciated her attention to detail and desire to do the job right, so I humbly followed her lead and made sure to cross all my T's and dot all my I's. She was very energetic and sometimes rough in her speech, but I did as she said and tried to learn all she had to teach me. She often delivered strong criticism when I didn't do things the specific way she wanted them. I took note and created a list of absolute no-nos that I would refrain from doing.

Soon I noticed that no matter how many mistakes I corrected, she always found more.

As my training proceeded, she had me listen to customer calls so I would understand how to handle them. It didn't take long for me to become concerned about her approach with customers. She often put them down based on how they handled conflict and whether they had created their own problems. After I observed her calls for a few weeks, I then had the opportunity to handle calls. I found that most of our customers needed guidance, so I gently guided them through the steps to fix their issues, assuring them that their mistakes were simply based on a need for more information about the way the industry works. The more my trainer saw how customers responded to my gentler, more positive approach, the angrier she became. Who was I to set a different standard?

When the tension between us rose to an unbearable pitch, I approached our general manager and said I wasn't sure the arrangement was going to work. I filled her in on the state of affairs, but emphasized that I did not want to make waves and would be happy to simply transfer if another position was open. One thing I didn't understand then was that when an employee brings a problem to a manager, that employee has little control over how the manager will solve it.

Instead of transferring me, the manager transferred my coworker. What's more, she transferred her to an area with very little customer contact and promoted me to take over her role. My coworker (and trainer) was shocked. She wasn't sure if it was a promotion or a reprimand. I could tell she blamed me for the change. Our relationship was never the same after that. I had burned the bridge with her for good, and possibly with anyone else to whom she might care to tell her version of the story. Not only that, I created an awkward atmosphere in a place where I still had to continue working for the next few years.

In retrospect, I probably should have done more to work with that colleague, tapping into her more reasonable side and seeking opportunities to let her shine in her own way. Under that rough exterior, she might have been more approachable and capable of resolving our conflict than I gave her credit for. At the time, I didn't think it was an option, partly because she seemed so attached to the drama, and partly because we needed to get business done at a fast pace. Keeping the goal of not burning bridges in the forefront of my mind might have guided me to a different conclusion.

"Anger is an acid that can do more harm to the vessel in which it is stored than to anything on which it is poured."
— Mark Twain

Creating Optimal Outcomes

The situation with my trainer started me on a path of realizing that it is important to predict outcomes and handle situations with the goal of preserving all people involved. My ultimate goal is to create a win-win solution whenever possible. Creative solutions are optimal, but win-wins are ideal. I have found that the wisest approach to creating any solution is to employ analysis, insight, and forethought to help me predict potential human reactions and the resulting systemic outcomes.

The key to conflict resolution is to keep my eye on the ball, striving my best to contribute in a positive way while working toward mutual goals.

"The only reason people burn bridges is because they let their ego take control and try to feed it."
— Grandma Valentine

In the years since I learned that first lesson about burning bridges, wisdom has taught me many alternatives for handling a difficult person: 1) be grateful I'm not that person, 2) focus on the task at hand, 3) maintain a respectful demeanor, 4) don't engage with that person at his level, 5) make an effort to avoid that type of difficult person as much as possible in future, thereby completely sidestepping the bridge so there's no chance of burning it.

When I have the strength to walk away from difficult people, I feel a lot happier. Grandma frequently reminded me of this "natural" outcome. I do not need to feed my ego to feel successful and happy. So I do not focus on proving that I can handle anything, and I do not focus on winning disputes. Instead, I prefer the gift of focusing my mind on thoughts and plans that lead me to greater purpose and fulfillment. I've found that that's the best way to produce optimal outcomes.

Clear Emotion From Analysis

I often called Grandma to tell her what was going on in my life, but I always called her when I was emotionally upset about something. Usually what upset me most was this: "Grandma, I'm worried I'm not doing what I should be doing, or what I want to be doing." I also often called Grandma when I was upset with someone. Mostly, I called Grandma because I wanted her to help me recognize when I was on the wrong path and when I was on the right one. I didn't want to accidentally burn a bridge that I didn't see standing right in front of me.

Grandma always appreciated humility, and I was humble enough to admit, "I don't know what to do!"

That's when she would help me put the brakes on: "Wait a minute, stop, slow down. Be very careful when you're upset. That's when damage is done. You can't back up and change that."

I didn't always give in to her wisdom right away. I'm usually a pretty easygoing person, with a high tolerance for people with different opinions and a long fuse for people who make mistakes. So if I was very unhappy with someone, it was usually because I was facing a person who was behaving in such a terrible way that it was doing potentially serious damage to relationships, reputations, and projects. In that sort of case, my goal was to remove the issue and/or person from the situation.

Grandma was just as incensed by terrible behavior as I was, but when I told her that I wanted to abruptly quit something, confront someone, or walk away in frustration, she would say, "Don't do it. Don't do it, because there's little value in doing it. The bad behavior will continue with or without you." She taught me that when a situation does not fit my values, I need to either find ways to work around the situation while maintaining my integrity, or leave with calm civility and find a position, person, or situation that does fit my values.

Very early in my career, I learned that we all need safety valves: people to whom we can vent our frustration who are in no way associated with our employers or colleagues, people from whom we don't have to fear repercussions. I always knew that if I called Grandma, she would be that confidential advisor.

Grandma was wise enough to understand that I needed to get the frustration resolved before I came to a conclusion. It was okay to be upset, because it would prompt me to recognize a need for change. But it wasn't okay to decide how to approach that change while I was still in a frustrated state. If I made a choice while I was angry, I would not be able to maintain the clarity necessary to consider all my options and all the possible consequences. This ability ties back to emotional homeostasis and the importance of being able to remove emotion to make rational judgments and decisions.

So Grandma would listen until I started repeating myself. That's when she would tell me to slow down, because that was the time to start letting go of my frustration and getting back my perspective. The thing she always said to diffuse my frustration was pretty simple: "Let it go and make a choice. There are only two options: stay or leave." She would suggest that if I decided to stay because I needed the job, then I needed to figure out how to remove emotion from the situation. On the other hand, if I had to leave, then I needed to make sure I knew what steps to take to move my career in the direction I wanted. Often I needed to find a balance point between the two: figure out how to remove emotion from the situation, so that I could stay long enough to accomplish what I needed while I looked for a new job.

Many new psychological studies suggest that frustration can contribute positively to decision-making. I'm not entirely disputing that idea. Various university studies have indicated that anger can: 1) stimulate the brain to better analyze data, 2) motivate someone to actually get off the dime and make a decision, 3) help a frustrated person feel more powerful and in control of her situation, and 4) give others the perception that the angry person is highly competent and in command—although it turns out that last effect is only true for men, not women, who are often perceived as incompetent and out-of-control when they display anger. Here's an important thing to realize about the way many of those studies were conducted: *first* anger was induced in the research subjects, *then* they were asked to analyze information, and *then* they were asked to make decisions. In other words, although anger was part of the decision process, the study subjects typically didn't make a decision during the height of their anger. They made it right afterward. Not to mention, while it's possible to study someone who feels *angry*, it's not too feasible to study someone in the midst of *blind rage*. So I stick by what Grandma says.

Maintaining Choices

Sometimes other people act so unreasonably that we feel tempted to fight or flee, but here's the thing: once you choose one of those, all your other choices are taken from you. Analyzing all available choices is a key component to approaching situations wisely. Putting a sense of calm into a hot situation allows for the development of a sensible plan. That plan might not only get you through the day, or the week, but also help get you to your next goal.

Sometimes the only way we can live with frustrating people and situations is by setting the anger aside long enough to create a new goal and a plan to achieve it. Having a plan can make frustration bearable, and sometimes it can even make anger disappear.

If you're sitting still, a mosquito on your arm can drive you crazy, but if you're racing in the Tour de France, you're so focused on pedaling that a mosquito seems inconsequential.

It's not always possible to know what choices to make to succeed in life. If we want wisdom to guide us in the decision process, we need to create the proper atmosphere for wisdom to operate. We limit our choices when we allow frustration to make us act impulsively instead of giving ourselves a chance to pause and think. We see more options when we let go of anxiety and return to calm. Whatever choices we make, the ones we make from that place of emotional homeostasis are more likely to be the right ones.

What Would Grandma Valentine Say?

There will always be people who build their success at the expense of others. The best way around them is not to let them distract your efforts.

A Step Toward Wisdom

Don't act rashly, at the height of anger. Act rationally, after channeling your frustration into the motivation to make a change.

The Wisdom of Reflecting

"It is not by muscle, speed, or physical dexterity that great things are achieved, but by reflection, force of character, and judgment."
– Marcus Tullius Cicero

Decisions Shape Who We Become

The path to wisdom is lined with pools for reflection, pools in which we regularly look to evaluate ourselves and our relationship to the world around us. I always tell my girls to reflect on their actions, as a way of helping them build the store of wisdom they'll need in their adult lives. When they have to make critical choices in life that I know they're going to revisit again and again, I have them stop for a moment and reflect on what they value and what their goals are. I want them to consider how each decision affects their actions, how each action reflects their values and goals, and how results are tied to those actions. I want them to understand that valuing something in their minds is meaningless unless they act on it. We are not the sum of our thoughts, we are the sum of our choices.

Ethical choices start with right thinking, but they don't end there. They end with action. Wanting to be good is not enough, unless you take the actions required to do good.

We learn the value of our actions through results, through the positive or negative consequences of our actions. When I talk about consequences, I'm not only talking about the way the world reacts to us, or the way it rewards or punishes us. Sometimes the world can be corrupt, so external rewards are only part of the picture. That's why self-reflection is important. Making choices helps us express who we are, so if we like who we are after we make a choice, and if that person is someone we're proud to be, that's a positive consequence. How we feel about ourselves is a consequence of our actions. Self-reflecting helps us understand that process.

It's important to not only reflect on ourselves, but also on the situations we face, and on how our choices in those situations will affect others. There is a difference between *worrying* about what other people think of us, and *caring* about how they feel. Worrying about what other people think can tempt us to do whatever will make us popular. But caring about how other people feel is a component of empathy. It reminds us not to seek popularity, but to do what will benefit both others and ourselves. This is one way to begin the social networking that is so important to every aspect of our lives. When we show concern for others, we build a foundation of people more likely to support us in our time of need. It's also simply the right thing to do.

Wisdom shows us that every action we take affects someone else, while other people's actions also affect us, so we really are all in this together. We are connected to each other. Reflection allows us to take a moment to see those connections. If I make a particular choice at work, how will it affect the work I produce, how will it affect my supervisor and colleagues, how will it affect my family, how will it affect me and the way I see myself as a professional, and how will it affect my future? If I make a particular choice at home, how will it affect my relationship with my husband and children, how will it affect our future, how will it take me closer to or further from the kind of wife and mother I would most like to be?

Reflect on More than One Choice

When I teach my children to reflect on the many threads of value, action, and consequence involved in their choices, I also try to get them to understand how those choices affect other people and their relationships with those people. Perfect example: One afternoon my older daughter, Brooke, came home from school and said, "Mommy, I don't want to go figure skating tonight. I will only go to the morning session." She said that she had too much homework to do, and there was no way she could do both skating sessions and finish her homework, so she had to give up something. In her mind that was the only option.

I believed that was a mistake.

Brooke's initial decision process represents a common mistake among adults as well, as discovered by Professor Paul Nutt of Ohio State University's Fisher College of Business, a leading expert on organizational decision-making. When leadership teams consider strategic decisions, how many alternatives do you think they consider? Nutt discovered that 70% of the time they consider only one. He also found evidence that those who simply add a second alternative improve their decisions dramatically. In one study, the leaders of a technology firm were asked to look back at decisions they had made ten years earlier and decide which ones had good outcomes. It turned out that the decisions in which a team had considered two alternative solutions or ideas were six times more likely to make their list of successes.

Luckily for Brooke, experience had taught me what Professor Nutt's research had taught him. As a businesswoman, I've had many opportunities to discover that there is rarely just one answer to consider. What's more, as a person for whom values are important, I know that I have to factor my values into every decision process.

I have to admit that my daughter's initial desire to choose homework over skating showed me that I was dealing with a child who does have great values. She just wasn't sure how to apply them when she had two values that came in conflict with each other. She believed she couldn't keep both commitments, so she was trying to prioritize: school comes first. Great choice! In this case, my values told me that my daughter should not turn this into an either-or proposition. Homework is important, but so is keeping commitments with other people, and so is having a well-rounded life in which we seek excellence in arenas outside the classroom or workplace. I didn't need a lot of time to process this because, unlike my daughter, I've been through dilemmas like this before, so I already had a store of wisdom on the subject.

I said something like, "Well, we have a problem because you cannot simply skip skating. You have to go. First of all, we've promised your coach that we'll come to both sessions, tonight and tomorrow morning. We knew this in advance and we're committed. So unless you're lying in a hospital somewhere, you go and don't waste his time. Second of all, we paid for the session, and you're not going to waste money. So you're going. You don't just decide you're not going to meet your commitments."

I wanted to show her that she didn't have to accept defeat right away, that if we are creative we can usually find a way to keep all our commitments. Of course, there's also an aspect of this issue that says, "Don't over-commit in the first place," but we weren't there yet. It was just a skating lesson and some homework, not a plethora of scheduling conflicts. So I said, "Oh boy, we have to figure out a plan that lets you do both."

"I'm never going to finish!" she cried. Her emotional state was upset. No homeostasis there. She was panicked, sure she couldn't face so much without failing. The emotion was raw, it was irrational, it was everything you would expect from a ten-year-old.

I remained calm and said, "Let's break it down."

Getting children to reflect and plan is not easy. They often have not done it before, or have not done it with great frequency, so they have no idea how powerful a little planning is. For many young people, it's just another boring task adults have invented to make their lives difficult. When I started to outline the things she needed to accomplish, Brooke didn't pay attention at first. Instead, she thumbed through the *Home Decorators* catalog on the kitchen counter, then meandered over to the couch in the family room and started playing with one of her sister's toys. She was mentally checking out. I don't give up so easily. I just saw this as another opportunity to teach her the importance of reflection.

"Okay," I said. "So you're the person with the homework emergency, but you have the time to do other things that aren't important. That tells me it's not really an emergency."

"Oh, but it is! I wasn't goofing off that long."

"If you have limited time, then every moment is going to count. So do you want me to help you work this out or not?"

She finally became still and attentive.

"Okay, I have some experience with this. Mommy loses her energy late at night, and I'm pretty sure you will too. So we're going to have to do a little bit of this homework before you go skating. You won't be able to finish all of it, but we'll see how much we can get done because we don't stay up late doing our homework. We'll fit it within the time we have. So we'll get maybe one-third to one-half of it done before tonight's skating session, then you'll come home, have dinner, do just a little more, and then go to sleep, because sleep is just as important as homework. Without sleep you'll be no good at school."

I was on a roll, because I was a mom who had experience with solving similar problems with work projects that conflicted with other commitments. "Next, I'm going to wake you up extra early in the morning, when we're fresh, and then we'll complete your homework. We'll prep for your quiz in the car on the way to skating, and by the time you get to school your homework and quiz prep will be done!"

She gave me a few, "But Mom...".s.

Because I had more experience than her, I had a solution ready for each "but." Then, before she could think of more obstacles, I quickly concluded, "Having a plan feels good, doesn't it?"

She wasn't convinced. I heard in the distance as I walked upstairs, "Oh my gosh, I'm never going to finish!"

I made sure she stuck with the plan. I understood that the reason she was still so freaked out was that she had never been through this experience before. I had. And once I helped her get through it, she would have this experience under her belt too. So she would feel more confident the next time, and less likely to insist on a dramatic scene.

At bedtime, when she still wasn't done, she was really upset, especially because as the night got later, the homework got harder and she was more tired. It is not easy to maintain emotional homeostasis when you're tired. So I said, "We'll sleep on it, and because you've had some sleep the homework will be easier in the morning."

So we slept on it, and when we got up at five in the morning everything went like clockwork. She ended up having to do part of the homework in the car on the way to her morning session. On the way back from skating, instead of playing her favorite music in the car like we usually did, we focused on prepping for her quiz, making the most of every second she had—the way adults do when they're under a deadline. When we got back to the house, we made sure the last piece of homework was in place. We finished with some fifteen minutes to spare.

Wise People Reflect on Decisions Before and After

When Brooke finished her homework, we weren't finished with the process of reflection. If this lesson was going to be meaningful, it was important to stop and reflect on what she had learned. I'm not talking about her school lesson, but the lesson about balancing commitments. So I made her stop and just sit still for a moment.

"Brooke, now stop and think about all that you just accomplished."

Her relief and feeling of accomplishment were tangible. She was grinning and laughing and clearly feeling good about herself.

I smiled and said, "See. You finished."

"Yeah! That was great, Mom. Thanks!" With that, she was ready to run out of the room and pack all her stuff in her backpack so we could head to school. But I could see that she had not yet thought about much beyond the fact that the nightmare was over.

So I said, "Stop, Brooke, really stop. Think about what you had facing you. What you had to do. What you were not willing to do." Then I reminded her, "In case you forgot, that means remembering that you had to go skating because you made a commitment, and that you were able to get everything done for school by staying focused and keeping your nose to the grindstone. You didn't let one moment escape without doing something to further your goal of finishing everything."

I could tell this seeming lecture made her a little uncomfortable. Children might roll their eyes at parents, or patiently endure us, but they do listen, and the lessons do creep in. I knew this was true because I had seen the evidence many times, including the night before: she had already decided homework was important, and where do you think she learned that?

So after this brief reminder of all the ups and downs of the past evening and morning I asked, "Now, do you feel good?"

"Yes."

"And do you feel calm, like you're ready to take on the day?"

"Yes."

"Do you feel prepared?"

"Yes."

"Now we've reflected on the moment, so you'll remember what to do the next time something like this happens in your life."

"Okay, Mommy."

So she made it to school, and not only was her homework done, but she did very well on her quiz preparing for that had been part of the homework. Instead of a day overshadowed by the disappointment of missing skating or failing to do her best at school, she had a lovely Friday, both at school and at home with her family that evening.

I've learned that after any success, big or small, it's important to take a moment for self-reflection, so you don't forget what it took to get to that moment. That moment of reflection will stop Brooke the next time she comes home and is tempted to say, "Oh, my gosh! I can't meet my previous commitment because I have a new commitment, so I'm going to excuse myself from my responsibility." Now she'll have an experience to draw from to help her overcome the next obstacle. Each time she does that it will make her stronger as a person of character who uses her wisdom to solve problems.

My Grandma often reminded me to pause and congratulate myself for my accomplishments, not only because of all the hard work I'd done, but also because of how easy it can be to live from problem to problem and forget to stop and count the joy in between.

"It's good to reflect on your mistakes, so you don't make them again. But it's also good to reflect on what you do well, so you'll remember how to do it again."
– Grandma Valentine

Reflection Is Empty Without Values

Stopping to reflect allows us a moment to remember that some of our values are not negotiable. A wise person knows that. There are certain things a wise person knows they won't do, even if those things provide an easy, or even an expected, means to solve a problem. A wise person adopts certain principles and terms of engagement under which he consistently operates. What I was reminding Brooke of during the homework-versus-skating problem was that there are certain things a wise person does not give up lightly.

We cannot have wisdom without a framework of values. Those values are instilled in us by others when we're children. As we become adolescents and young adults we affirm or adjust those values. Then we revisit them as we grow and mature throughout life. If someone doesn't work on a personal ethical framework, and doesn't see each situation as an opportunity to build on that framework, then when a problem comes along it can seem hopeless or nearly impossible to solve. If you don't know your values, then how do you have a baseline against which to test your choices? If you don't know your values, how do you know which choices will carry you to emotional homeostasis, or when it's worthwhile to deviate from homeostasis and accept the need to face a conflict?

"Bitter experience has taught us how fundamental our values are and how great the mission they represent."
— Jan Peter Balkenende

Sometimes when we're not confident about how a choice fits into our values framework, we go to our version of the wise old man in the village and say, "I have this problem. Can you help me decide how to deal with it?" For me, that person used to be my grandma, and although she's gone now, she helped strengthen my framework to the point that I can now make most of those sorts of decisions on my own, though I often consult with my husband or other trusted friends and advisors. All of those people, including my internal self, are some version of the old wise man in the village.

In a mythical village long ago someone might have said to this wise old man something like, "My husband isn't finding enough food for me anymore, so I want to leave him."

The wise man might have replied, "Are you sure that's smart? Your husband might well be hunting in a field where all the animals have left, which is out of his control. And later, when he finds a different field full of animals, you might regret leaving your husband."

In other words, we often think we have an urgent matter we have to solve right this moment, because we're frustrated right now and feel a lack of control. We feel the urge to get back to homeostasis as soon as possible, but we haven't thought through the long-term consequences. The wise man or woman stops to ask, "Is the choice you want to make really going to achieve your goal in the long run?"

When we reflect, we consult our own inner wise man, or wise woman. We step back and think about the alternative ways we can use to gain some balance again. One of the things we consider as we look at those alternatives is the values framework we're striving to build and how each alternative might strengthen or weaken that framework. These decisions don't always happen quickly. When they do it's only because we, or the wise person we consult, has been through a similar situation in the past.

Wisdom Requires Patience

Wisdom involves plenty of patience, because it takes time to develop experience at dealing with problems. Even with experience, the need for patience does not diminish. Each individual problem poses unique challenges, which may require time to analyze in terms of making the best choice for our long-term well-being—not just the one that gives immediate gratification.

Another reason wisdom requires patience is because our decisions don't just involve ourselves, but also other people. That means we have to have a lot of patience for the human condition and human nature. We have to remember that other people might be counting on us to do what we say we're going to do. We also have to be prepared for how other humans might react to our choices or interact with those choices. That requires having patience with other people's weaknesses, and with their untold stories—in other words, there might be hidden reasons for their reactions that they cannot explain to us.

Reflecting on Human Nature

When I talk about human nature, it's tempting to think of it as a mystery. But as we gather experience in making choices, we begin to notice that these choices often result in recurring reactions from other people. Some reactions are positive, some negative, but the variety of responses often reveals consistent patterns that we can learn to recognize and predict.

When I was consulting for large corporations, our consulting team would be paired up with another team comprised of people from various functional areas of the corporation. Sometimes, working with a consulting team added stress to the work lives of the corporate employees, which would manifest itself in frustration and impatience about the project. To soften this impact, we gave assessments to the team to identify their different working styles, and I always tried to keep in mind their different temperaments as I worked with them. I happily took on the employees who were the most pressured, because I had spent time in corporate America and understood some of their stress.

I remember one gentleman I worked with who was stressed by the project, worrying that his participation would take away time from his "regular" job. I was asked to pair up with him and support him through the project. This was an opportunity to win his heart and mind so that he could experience the good feeling that comes from successful project work.

Our group went on our first research trip, and we divvied up the research responsibilities among two-person teams. I was paired up with the stressed gentleman. Our team's job was to gather data on people through personal interviews. Some of the folks we interviewed were pretty colorful. I took the attitude that these people represented exciting opportunities for new experiences. At least, that's what I told my partner the day one inebriated man from the bayou began playfully brandishing his unloaded Colt revolver as he proudly shared stories of his wild ways. I took comfort from the presence of his sober and watchful friend, and decided that the inebriated man was sloppy and harmless. He was simply trying to show us visitors how exciting his part of the country was. However, although I was undaunted, I wasn't foolish. I took safety precautions and considered exit strategies. I made sure my partner and I were not in the line of fire and that there was a barricade of furniture between us and him in case the gun had a bullet in the chamber. The bottom line was: we were there for a purpose, so I held firm and focused on getting the data we required. My partner stood silently by my side, in complete disbelief.

As we drove away, I said, "See how many unique and interesting experiences you'll be able to collect on this project?"

He laughed heartily as he said how crazy it was for us to stay and finish collecting data as opposed to running out the door as fast as possible. This signaled a transformation in his thought process. Whatever untold story of his that had driven his reluctance to be part of our project team was now crowded out by a crazy experience that would make this project unforgettable for him.

We had many other unique experiences as the project went on, because they were fueled by human interaction, which is ultimately unpredictable. But thanks to our shared experience with the Bayou Gunslinger, we had developed a new thought process that allowed us to relax and have a good time with each other and with the project. We saw that this truly wasn't just a job but an adventure, an adventure in the exploration of human nature: each other's, and that of the people we met.

Human nature is at the core of many difficult situations. So developing an understanding of human nature will strengthen your ability to manage your homeostasis in tough situations, assess what's needed, and make decisions. "I've seen something like this before," you might say. "This is just history repeating itself. The best bet is to adhere to my values by choosing option A, and to avoid comprising my values by pursuing option B."

A situation may or may not repeat itself. I do my best to handle each new situation in accordance with my values and my desired outcome. Then I watch the results. If the results pass the test of adhering to my values and goals, then I'll know how to handle similar situations the next time. If they don't, then it's time to reflect on my response, and to consider what might have worked better while still allowing me to follow my values.

Whatever my reflections reveal to me about myself and my choices, I'm always waiting for the next opportunity to reapply a past approach or try a new one. Each time I make a new decision, it's a fresh opportunity to take my course closer and closer to the ideal goal of becoming the most ethical and successful human I'm capable of being.

What Would Grandma Valentine Say?

If you know what's important, then you know what to do.

A Step Toward Wisdom

Wisdom is not a place we arrive, it is a path we walk, and that path is lined with pools in which we look and reflect on ourselves.

8

Wise People Know What They Value

"The men and women who have the right ideals…are those who have the courage to strive for the happiness which comes only with labor and effort and self-sacrifice, and those whose joy in life springs in part from power of work and sense of duty."
– Theodore Roosevelt

What Is a Value?

Even though most people have beliefs, ideals, and desires, as well as people, places, and things that are important to them, many would be hard-pressed to identify their values. I believe that if you don't give thought to what you most value in yourself and others, aside from money or power, you'll probably have a hard time making big decisions, setting and achieving meaningful goals, or having a sense of purpose in life. Part of growing in wisdom is looking both within ourselves and around us, to identify what we embrace as valuable and worth our effort versus what we reject as unworthy of our energy or time.

Sometimes people reject the idea of developing wisdom because the choices they perceive as wise don't always lead to the ends they desire. People who want the quickest and easiest means to an end may well get what they believe they want, but they're likely to find themselves dissatisfied when they get it. If I didn't know what I valued, I would have no idea who I was. I would be a stranger to myself.

We all spend more of our lives moving toward our goals than we do in our brief moments of victory. If our values don't guide us on the path, our lives will not reflect who we want to be, no matter what we achieve.

"Act as if the maxim of your action were to become by your will a general law of nature."
– Immanuel Kant

One of the first steps toward wisdom is to know what you value. I have found it helpful to write down the actions, ideals, and beliefs that I value the most. Some people incorporate their values in a personal or family mission statement. The physical act of writing things down helps consolidate them in our memories. When we know by heart what we value, then making decisions doesn't take as long. Further, if you know what you value, it is easier to decide the proper course of action that will keep you on the right path.

Understanding what you value requires the self-reflection I spoke of in Chapter Seven. When it came time for my daughter Brooke to decide whether or not to go to her skating lesson, I reminded her of a value that I knew was important for her to have: keeping her commitments. In the future it will be easier for her to decide on a course of action in similar situations where she has a schedule conflict, because she'll be able to tie her decision back to that value. Most importantly, her value tells her that if she fails to keep her commitments she'll be letting herself down. Over time that will become one of the values that defines her.

Understanding what we value gives us the strength to do whatever we have to do to stay on the path toward becoming the best version of ourselves.

When we're growing up, we learn many of our foundational values from our elders: parents, grandparents, teachers, and mentors. If we're lucky, most of them are good values that we'll want to keep. Our elders demonstrate their values through what they do, explain the meaning behind their values through what they say, and give us experience in practicing their values by sometimes guiding or correcting our behavior. As we mature, we expand and develop our own values, by blending what we've learned from our elders with what we learn from our peers, from experience, and from self-reflection. In the end, each of us will have a list of values that's unique to us, although if we're true to our best selves we're sure to attract others who have similar values, or who at least appreciate the path of wisdom as we do.

Benjamin Franklin's 13 Virtues

According to Benjamin Franklin's unfinished autobiography, when he was only twenty years old he created a system of guidelines to develop his character. His system boiled down to a list of thirteen virtues designed to guide him to practical habits that he believed would result in becoming an increasingly better man. He created a chart to measure his progress in each virtue, and carried the list of virtues in his pocket. They served as a daily reminder of the code he lived by, guiding his daily actions and choices. Here's the list Franklin carried with him:

Benjamin Franklin's 13 Virtues

1. **Temperance:** Eat not to dullness; drink not to elevation.

2. **Silence:** Speak not but what may benefit others or yourself; avoid trifling conversation.

3. **Order:** Let all your things have their places; let each part of your business have its time.

4. **Resolution:** Resolve to perform what you ought; perform without fail what you resolve.

5. **Frugality:** Make no expense but to do good to others or yourself; i.e., waste nothing.

6. **Industry:** Lose no time; be always employed in something useful; cut off all unnecessary actions.

7. **Sincerity:** Use no hurtful deceit; think innocently and justly, and, if you speak, speak accordingly.

8. **Justice:** Wrong none by doing injuries, or omitting the benefits that are your duty.

9. **Moderation:** Avoid extremes; forebear resenting injuries so much as you think they deserve.

10. **Cleanliness:** Tolerate no uncleanness in body, clothes, or habitation.

11. **Chastity:** Rarely use venery but for health or offspring, never to dullness, weakness, or the injury of your own or another's peace or reputation.

12. **Tranquility:** Be not disturbed at trifles, or at accidents common or unavoidable.

13. **Humility:** Imitate Jesus and Socrates.

Source: "Benjamin Franklin: An American Life" by Walter Issacson, Simon & Schuster Paperbacks, 2004, pp. 89-90.

Grandma Valentine's 11 Values

My grandma did not write down her list of virtues, which I call values, but she and I spoke of them often and I know that she kept them before her mind's eye at all times. Grandma's values guided all her actions and all her advice to me. Because Grandma's philosophies about life, human nature, and wisdom resonated so strongly with me, her values became the foundation for mine. I heard her repeat her values so often that it's easy for me to remember them at will. But to ensure I never forget them, and to share them with you, I've written a list of her key values, of which there are eleven. Here's the short version, followed by an explanation of each:

Grandma Valentine's 11 Values

1) Wisdom knows no boundaries.

2) Self-reliance is the backbone of the spirit.

3) Appreciate all you have, and everyone has something to appreciate.

4) Practice truth and decorum.

5) Don't burn bridges.

6) Don't romanticize the good old days.

7) Don't judge character by what people say, but by what they do.

8) Stay positive.

9) Keep everything in perspective.

10) Humility is the most desirable character trait.

11) A sense of duty is critical.

1) Wisdom knows no boundaries.

Wisdom does not have a price tag or physical limit. For ten years of my emerging adulthood, my patient grandma simply helped me connect people and situations to values and ideals, and to reflect on the connections between external reality and my internal values system. Grandma used the Socratic method, though I'm not sure she would have called it that, answering my questions with more questions that would help me engage in the kind of critical thinking by which I could shape my own personal philosophy. Grandma believed that there are answers to almost every human problem, but she understood that not everyone wants to know the answers. To her, a wise person is willing to press as far and as deep as necessary to find the answers that will help her create solutions to benefit others and herself.

2) Self-reliance is the backbone of the spirit.

The way my grandma saw it, self-reliance might begin with something as simple as relying on yourself to do what needs to be done to make sure you have food, shelter, and rest—but it results in so much more. She taught me that it is the spirit of self-reliance that brings people through hard times, and that in turn, living through hard times strengthens that spirit. When she looked around her own neighborhood and witnessed people trapped in generational cycles of welfare, accompanied by low self-esteem and lack of self-reliance, she told me that their spirit was broken. Grandma was a charitable person, but she believed that welfare programs needed a component that taught people what they needed to know to become self-sufficient.

3) Appreciate all you have, and everyone has something to appreciate.

Grandma was a young woman during the Great Depression and she was what many people might call poor, but she still remained content. She believed that as long as she had her health, the ability to work, and people around her to love, then she had plenty to be thankful for. She spent her energies taking care of others, and she appreciated the opportunity to do so. When others did things for her, that was icing on the cake, and she appreciated that. Everyone she knew shared what they had, not just in terms of possessions, but in deeds. She appreciated that too. She did not dwell on what was lacking, but focused on what was abundant. Grandma believed that appreciation, especially appreciation of others, is at the core of true happiness.

"The roots of all goodness lie in the soil of appreciation for goodness."
– Dalai Lama

Grandma believed that if you wanted to feel the full benefits of appreciation, the best way was to express your gratitude to others. She deeply appreciated receiving handwritten thank you cards, an art that seems to be dying but one well worth reviving. Think about how much it means to you when someone takes the time to write you a formal thank you. It is that person's selfless acknowledgment of your importance to him or her, a way of saying that you make a difference in his or her life. In turn, it makes you feel gratitude toward that person. In that way, appreciation is exponential, the gift that keeps on giving. You've heard the saying, "You don't know what you've got till it's gone." Grandma never wanted to risk that kind of regret, so she made it a daily practice to remind herself of all she had.

When Grandma measured a person's character, one important measure was how much appreciation that person demonstrated. If someone complained a lot, Grandma would dismiss that person—though she did so politely, so that the other person probably never knew.

Grandma went out of her way to do kind and generous things for people, and she never asked for anything in return. She didn't keep score, because she believed that the good things in her life were gifts and that doing for others was her way of giving back. It didn't matter if those people weren't responsible for the gifts in her life. The way she saw it, we're all in this together, so what you put out there comes back to you, and what comes to you must be put back out there.

Grandma's style of appreciation was not just about gifts or gestures, but also about treating people with consideration and respect. One of her most beautiful ways of showing appreciation was to listen to people with opinions different from her own, to let them express themselves without trying to make them wrong. She believed that if she kept her mind open she just might learn something. That ability, to appreciate what other people had to offer even if they were offering something she didn't agree with, was one of her most beautiful virtues.

4) Practice truth and decorum.

My grandma believed in behaving with dignity under all circumstances. Whenever I came to her to discuss work problems, she made it clear to me, "Don't react in an unprofessional manner, no matter how big a problem you're having." Even when I came to her with personal relationship problems, she suggested that no matter how much someone else hurt me it was no reason to lose control of myself. That's not to say that she expected me to behave like some robot that never cried or got angry, but that I could express those things without launching into dramatics or crazy behavior. Whatever the world might do to me, it was important to remember who I was and not let it impact my reaction.

"To bear defeat with dignity, to accept criticism with poise, to receive honors with humility—these are marks of maturity and graciousness."
— William Arthur Ward

Although my grandma had strong beliefs, no one would have called her opinionated. She spoke carefully and thoughtfully. She understood how the human mind could alter the most innocent of comments into something unintended and unforgivable. In this age of the Internet and mass media, I notice that it almost seems expected that people will call each other names, say things that they assume to be true without any evidence or firsthand knowledge, or take it upon themselves to over-simplify and expound upon complex topics about which they know little or nothing.

Grandma respected people who thought before they spoke, and who only remarked on things about which they were knowledgeable. Even when I told her about my run-ins with people I'd witnessed behaving unfairly to others, she cautioned me to keep any insulting terms or assumptions out of the story. She put truth and decorum hand-in-hand, because when you make emotional assumptions about the truth it's tempting to stray from the facts. That's when one's behavior can become dramatic, disrespectful, or unreasonable. When people accept and spread glorified opinions or spiteful gossip as the truth, there is nothing dignified about that.

Grandma appreciated facts. She appreciated people who had the courage to be honest about all sides of a story, especially when one of those sides wasn't flattering to them. She did not translate the idea of truth and decorum into political correctness. To her, political correctness was too far to the other extreme: preventing people with different ideas from engaging in healthy debate and possibly developing a deeper understanding and appreciation for each other's point of view.

5) Don't burn bridges.

Grandma gave me this piece of advice most often for work-related situations, but it applies to personal lives as well. I have met difficult people along the way who made me want to confront them, ignore them, or entirely leave the situation that brought us into contact. Grandma didn't tell me to let go of any of those options. She just suggested I ask myself the question: "If you take that course of action, will you burn a bridge with someone who's important to you now or who might be important to you later?" "Don't burn bridges" has taught me that in some situations I have to find ways to live with personality differences, or even unfortunate actions by others, because there are some situations in which responding just won't help anybody.

6) Don't romanticize the good old days.

Things were not better yesterday than they are today, at least in terms of the human condition. Humanity has not changed that much. Researchers have compiled significant data to suggest we're probably less violent than we were earlier in human history. But just because modern humans engage in less violence does not change the fact that we're capable of violence. From the beginning, there have always been people without wisdom who take all the shortcuts to get what they want: violence, theft, dishonesty, and all manner of corruption.

In 1915, when Grandma was five years old, a man chased her down the alley with a potato sack in the hope of kidnapping her. She was fast and clever, and she avoided capture. Years later, whenever she heard on the news that a child had been abducted her heart would sink. "The poor darling got caught," she would say. But she was never surprised, by anything from kidnapping to religious wars. "People don't change much," she told me. "This sort of thing has been going on for a very long time."

"When people look at the past as if it's better than today, they're using selective memory. Human nature has not changed all that much over the years."
– Grandma Valentine

The reason the advice of a woman in her eighties and nineties served me so well in my twenties and thirties is precisely because people don't change all that much. In Grandma's mind, human behavior was just as predictable in 1915 as it is now.

The only two major differences Grandma saw between her time and mine were: 1) the advancement of technology, which she and I agreed was generally a good and miraculous thing; and 2) the decreased quality of fruits and vegetables, which we agreed was due to human intervention and the desire for shortcuts. Grandma was convinced that corporate farms were not rotating crops enough to allow for the replenishment of soil nutrients. She was upset when triple-A butter was nowhere to be found in the 1980s. But people? She was certain people had not changed much. The same motivations that drive people to be greedy or cruel today were in place long ago, mainly the desire for wealth and power without a values framework. The players change, but the actions and the outcomes are predictable.

Today we certainly have more access to bad news, what with the 24/7, around-the-world news cycle of the Internet and TV/cable networks. Years ago, people tended to rely more on local gossip for their bad news. Grandma stopped watching TV by the 1990s. For her, the media focused too much on the negative. She thought what little positive news received any play tended to be silly. Like the sorts of studies which show that if you don't eat, sleep, take care of yourself, and wash your hands, you're far more likely to get sick. Nothing like stating the obvious. Otherwise, she believed the modern news media focused on the dramatic, the catastrophic, and whatever had the greatest shock value. But even if we have more access to bad news than ever before, sensationalistic journalism has been around since the Penny Press, and people have been behaving sensationally badly since Cain killed Abel. Grandma understood that, and I still agree.

"You can clutch the past so tightly to your chest that it leaves your arms too full to embrace the present."
— Jan Glidewell

---

7) Don't judge character by what people say, but by what they do.

"To truly understand a person, don't just listen to what they say. Look at what they do, and don't explain it away or forget it." Grandma said that a lot. She was emphatic about that second sentence. She knew that when charismatic leaders made people believe in them with fancy words, it was tempting to explain away discrepancies in their actions, sometimes even developing amnesia about what they did if it contradicted what they said—or vice versa.

This subject mostly came up when Grandma and I talked about politicians. By the time she reached voting age in 1928, she was eager to cast her first vote. A quiet but firm advocate for women's rights, she never did understand why women had to fight so long for their right to vote. Although she was not the type to make speeches and draw attention to herself, if someone asked her opinion she was always firm in her belief that a woman's ideas were as valuable as a man's. And one of her ideas was that politicians should never make promises they wouldn't even try to keep. Grandma carefully followed elections and listened to what politicians said. She valued honesty and was deeply offended by liars, especially when their lies hurt people.

She was most disappointed by U.S. Presidents Lyndon Johnson and Richard Nixon. She had a special disdain for Johnson because he was unfaithful to his wife. She believed that someone who couldn't maintain loyalty and commitment in his most important personal relationship could not be trusted to maintain loyalty and commitment in his public life. It didn't matter to her that he promised a Great Society, because she wasn't listening just for what he promised to the electorate, but watching how he failed to keep his promise to his wife. In Grandma's book, someone whose words and actions didn't match was not to be trusted, period.

8) Stay positive.

Grandma had an anti-whining policy, which my mother largely adopted when she was raising my brothers and me. While Grandma understood the need for everyone to have someone in whom to confide, she found it selfish for a person to spend a lot of time generally complaining about personal problems, because everyone has his share of trouble. In a world full of people with wants and needs, staying positive seemed the only considerate option. In a way, it's another aspect of her belief in appreciation, but this aspect is all about attitude.

During the Depression, self-pity seemed a waste of time that Grandma knew could be better spent doing something to improve her situation or to help others. The tougher things got, the more important it was to avoid self-pity, which would only make her feel worse while dampening the spirits of everyone around her. In an uncertain world, a can-do attitude was the only option. It didn't guarantee results, but a *can't-do* attitude was a guarantee of no results.

"Courage doesn't always roar. Sometimes courage is the quiet voice at the end of the day saying, "I will try again tomorrow."
– Mary Anne Radmacher

My grandparents carried a can-do attitude throughout life, and it helped them achieve their goals. They toiled and pushed forward without complaint. That's how they stayed married for sixty-six years, bought a home, raised a healthy family, opened a Dog n' Suds, and watched several children and grandchildren go on to higher education and professional careers. Though they never became wealthy, they led full, happy lives. That's the power of a positive attitude.

Because Grandma worked through hard times with little more than a positive attitude and common sense, she never understood the self-help book craze. She could not for the life of her understand the focus on feelings and whether people were happy or sad. She felt that, for most people, happiness grew out of the attitude they chose to take. She and I sometimes discussed the idea that modern technology has taken over so many tasks once done by humans, that it gives people too much time to sit around pondering what they don't have, and too much opportunity to watch TV and envy what other people do have.

People who focus on doing, doing, doing—even in the evening when most people now watch TV—don't have time to worry about things they can do nothing about, or sulk about what they don't have. For grandma, a busy mind and body contributed to a positive spirit.

9) Keep everything in perspective.

Many situations in life are so complicated that they can seem downright impossible to work through. Grandma felt that sometimes the only answer was to make the best of it. Making the best of it doesn't always mean you'll resolve the situation. What it means is that you'll work toward the best possible outcome. It means that if the best possible outcome isn't what you hoped for, you'll remember to return to her value #4 and appreciate what you have.

Grandma liked to say, "Discipline of mind is my best friend. It helps me understand the basic value of anything and try to stay with that value, rather than worry about how it's dressed up." For example, if my goal is to buy a house, I could easily become disappointed if I can't afford the brand new mini-mansion that's my first choice. But I have to remember that the core value here is the opportunity to own my own home, even if it's an older, smaller house in need of some work. That's making the best of it, or in other words, that's keeping things in perspective.

To Grandma, keeping things in perspective also meant keeping appropriate timing in mind. Whenever I told her about something I was striving to achieve and I expressed worry that I hadn't achieved it yet, she'd say, "When the time is right." She was puzzled when people felt they had to achieve their goals as soon as they acted on them, instead of allowing for the circumstances, finances, people, and events to all fall into place when the timing was right. Whenever Grandma ran across people who had trouble keeping things in perspective, she believed that impatience was at the root of the problem. A patient person, Grandma always kept things in perspective. If she didn't achieve a goal right away, she kept pushing forward anyway, believing that things would fall into place at exactly the right time, and no sooner.

10) Humility is the most desirable character trait.

Both my grandma and my mom used to like to remind all of us kids, "The world does not revolve around you." It's a simple truth that I'm passing on to my children, too. If you truly care about yourself, you'll always take an interest in the troubles and achievements of others, because it is your inter-actions with the people and the world around you that allow you to grow as a person. A person who truly loves herself or himself must therefore be deeply humble.

I came to know about Grandma's admiration of humility largely thanks to her head-shaking comments about the excesses of the 1980s, which she found so much more pronounced than the budding new privileges of the 1950s. The eighties drove her crazy! It was a decade of flaunting riches and clout, which turned her off. A few of her passing comments about strangers, celebrities, and politicians: "That's too flashy," or "No good use of judgment," or "I don't like how that person comes off—too much, too much."

Such comments underlined that humility was the trait she admired most. Humility reflected people who cared about truly being themselves more than trying to prove themselves to someone else. Arrogance usually required a certain amount of pretentiousness or phoniness. In short, someone who lacked humility was usually a boaster. In grandma's eyes, such a person could not be trusted.

11) A sense of duty is critical.

Duty is all about keeping our commitments. Some of these duties are spoken or written down, such as commitments to take a class, pay a bill, honor marriage vows, or perform a job for an employer or a client. But other duties are unspoken or implied, such as the duty to teach our children right from wrong, to take care of an ailing parent, to listen to a friend who is going through hard times. A sense of duty helps us know what to do when our wants and needs conflict with the wants and needs of others. Is what the other person asks of us an imposition, or are they calling on our sense of duty?

For me, the most poignant example of a sense of duty was when I told my employer I would be unavailable because my grandmother needed me to stay with her for a weekend. It never occurred to me to worry about whether my employer would judge me for not being committed enough to my job. That's partly because up to that moment in time I had diligently served my employer with a sense of duty, always working to one hundred percent of my ability to achieve project goals.

I've had the opportunity to answer my internal call of duty many times, and it always gives me even greater gifts in return. I remember flying back to Chicago several years ago to help my mom recover from shoulder surgery. I feel that sitting by a loved one's side during a crisis makes a big difference, even if there's not a lot for us to do. By keeping my mother's spirits up, advocating to make sure her needs were met, and making her comfortable, I believe I was doing my part to help reduce the stress of recovery and speed up her healing process. I sensed she was relieved to have the support and company. And in the end, it was fun to hang out with my mom, to take the opportunity to bond and enjoy a few quiet moments between us.

I know that if I follow my sense of duty, or commitment, at all times, I'll always end up where I'm supposed to be, with the people I'm supposed to be with, doing what I'm supposed to be doing.

My Values Don't Negate Yours

You'll notice that Grandma Valentine's 11 Values and Ben Franklin's 13 Virtues don't precisely match up, though I would be surprised if you didn't find both lists worthy of consideration. Many other values, such as hard work, respect, and courage, are sewn through everything my husband and I do with our daughters. It's likely you have values that are more important to you than those listed in this chapter, or that you would translate some of the values I've described differently than I do. Maybe you prefer the idea of "realistic thinking" over "positive attitude," or maybe your views of charity put less of an emphasis on self-reliance and more on accepting that some people are not as capable as you. I respect that, because, like my grandma, I believe that we all have something to teach each other.

Knowing what you value does not negate what other people value. To praise one thing is not to damn another. Only you can determine your own values framework. It's not as critical what you value, as it is to decide to value *something*, because it is in practicing those values that you pave your own personal path to wisdom.

What Would Grandma Valentine Say?

How can you truly want anything, or be satisfied when you get it, if you don't know what you value?

A Step Toward Wisdom

Reflecting on your values is a means to discovering who you are so that you can make the choices in life that are right for you.

9

Wise People Don't Know Everything

"To invent, you need a good imagination and a pile of junk."
– Thomas A. Edison

The Value of the Educated Guess

Wisdom is not what you know as much as it is what you're willing to learn. That's why I don't feel the need to know everything before I dive into starting a project or solving a problem. Like many children, I spent most of my school years learning how to gather information. When I attended business school one of the most exciting, and relieving, things I learned was that I was most likely never going to enter into a problem, project, or decision for which I would have all the information. The key was to ascertain as much as I needed to know so that I could bring my talents to bear, and then fill in the blanks with the wisdom I had gained through experience and education. It was a simple but important notion that freed me from the constraints of hunting down complete information before making decisions. Discovering that having all the information is not a real-life requirement for success gives people permission to proceed the best they can with the information they have.

In modern business, many people put excessive faith in *big data*, that is, information technology and the massive data it can aggregate on everything from target demographics to the psychology behind purchasing decisions, from cost-benefit analysis to profit-and-loss projections. Although that information can be useful, that's not where all of the innovation comes from. Identifying the patterns within data can help, but innovation requires a large amount of creative thought and insight.

The biggest asset anyone brings to the table in any venture is not data. Far more valuable are creativity, intuition, imagination, leadership, and strategy—talents not easily quantified.

The founder of American Pragmatism, philosopher Charles Sanders Peirce (1839-1914), theorized that no new idea in the world was ever produced by either inductive or deductive reasoning. He believed that innovation required a third component: *abductive* reasoning, or making inferences from commonly known facts. At first, Peirce simply called this "guessing," but it's really more about creative hypothesizing. If you only test ideas that spring from what you know for certain, that means relying on what has been learned in the past. Peirce asserted that if we rely on the past for all our information, then we cannot create a future that's different from the past.

Another way of looking at Peirce's concept of abduction, is that the growth of knowledge can be squashed by relying too much on information-gathering. That's why the greatest scholars, inventors, and innovators typically become experts in narrow disciplines. Instead of trying to fatten their brains on stacks of previously known information about many things, they learn just a few things in depth, and leave the ordinary stuff that many of us call "common sense" to people of common intellect. That way they can leave more of their intellect unencumbered to engage in hypothesizing and imagining creative new ways to approach previously unaddressed problems, wants, or needs—or even to predict future problems, wants, or needs.

Abduction is a form of using wisdom in that the use of wisdom allows for prediction. Using patterns and experience to guide oneself into the unknown is a key advantage of developing wisdom. World-class scholars, political leaders, and business moguls develop their specific expertise to a point that they may be weak in certain general areas. So they often fill in the blanks by delegating what they can and using their wisdom to intuit the rest.

What's miraculous about the human brain is not how great it is at memorizing. Any computer can do that. Rather, the miracle of the human brain is its ability to identify patterns, and to fill in the rest with imagination, educated guesses, and hunches. The innovation is in the places where you fill in the blanks. Put all that together and you have a more complete picture of wisdom.

According to a 2012 article in the *Harvard Business Review*, the business leadership consulting company Corporate

Executive Board evaluated five thousand employees at twenty-two global companies and sorted them into three groups: "unquestioning empiricists" who trust analysis over judgment, "visceral decision makers" who go exclusively with their gut, and "informed skeptics," whom CEB considers the employees best equipped to make good decisions. "Informed skeptics" have strong analytical skills, strike a balance between data analysis and intuitive judgment, and respect other people's opinions without being afraid to disagree.

Unfortunately CEB found that only 38% of employees and 50% of senior managers fell into the prized category of "informed skeptics." CEB identified that as one of the problems that prevent organizations from getting more bang for their buck out of big data. Apparently, whenever a new form of analytics enters a workplace, many companies will hire experts, reasoning that their skills will trickle down to everyone. Often the trickle doesn't travel far. CEB concluded that companies would do better to ensure that all of their employees are trained in using analytical skills, rather than just a select few. In other words, more companies would benefit from people who don't just eat and regurgitate data, but who know how to fill in the blanks with analytical thinking that leads to innovation.

Filling in the Blanks

I believe the need for greater creative analysis, that ability to balance information and ambiguity, is important in all areas of life. When you can fill in the blanks to solve disputes, conquer financial problems, and create exciting projects, you feel less like a lonely mouse in a maze and start to feel more like a contributor to your community, friends, and family.

Grandma loved hearing about the projects I became involved with when I was consulting, because the main focus of the projects was identifying white spaces (blank areas) for large companies. These companies represented a wide variety of industries with different challenges and opportunities. Grandma enjoyed my stories of dividing groups of people into the ideal mix of people to interview. Identifying the critical demographics and psychographics essential to get the right people into an interview seat was interesting to Grandma. It was also the ideal method for gathering new insights and ideas to capitalize on opportunities in different markets. To Grandma, this process was much bigger than big data. It was a way to learn different approaches to problems that may or may not be currently known or identified.

Filling in the blanks can be especially important when trying to identify specific areas of need across different groups of people. Some people interpret this sort of research as a specialized component of wisdom. I believe it qualifies as wisdom because it's a method of gaining higher-level understanding of situations and opportunities.

Certainty Can Limit Innovation

The challenge to letting go of certainty is that our brains have a survival skill of wanting to figure everything out or have all of the information as soon as possible. That's probably how our ancestors survived in the wild: able to quickly assess food, shelter, and tribal security versus dangerous plants and animals, exposure to weather, and potential enemies. In modern society, the trick is not to let ambiguity be a deterrent. All you need if you want to move forward is a willingness to listen, ask questions, learn, and implement.

Whether the project or problem you're dealing with is professional, personal, or communal, the most important question you can ask is: "How can I create or capture value in this situation?" In business you'll ultimately be held accountable for numbers and results, while in personal relationships you'll ultimately be held accountable for empathy and generosity. In either case, accepting some uncertainty is necessary if you want to keep moving forward.

Most people don't like ambiguity. I'm sure you know people who need to know every detail of a situation before they'll begin thinking about how to proceed. One of the benefits of well-developed wisdom is that it makes ambiguity manageable so that it is no longer a major source of anxiety or concern. Most people are not hungry to develop wisdom. They're mainly interested in quick solutions. Sidestepping the use of wisdom presents its own issues, such as lackluster choices, hit-or-miss luck, and a lost sense that our actions have meaning.

As a person learns to act intuitively, it builds self-confidence and the ability to rely on those instincts in future. Having to know every detail can stymie that ability. I've known people to allow missing information to paralyze them. They refuse to move without knowing every piece of information that has been processed and every single thing that has happened so far, so that they can predict what will happen in the future. Even if they had all that data, they would be unable to predict the future. Even if they had enough data to estimate a likely future, there is a great risk that it would resemble the past.

Taoists have an idea that the key to knowing is not knowing. The moment you think you know something, you've stopped growing and stopped learning. Questions are important. You have to ask questions if you're going to learn. However, you also need to know when it's time to stop asking and start inventing. The best things in life happen in that place of uncertainty, that place from which you have to make a leap of faith. Wise people know that.

For me, there's nothing more exciting than making a decision without knowing every detail, and then watching an innovative plan come together. Even if it fails, that too becomes useful data. The lessons of failure can teach you how to succeed next time.

Building Wisdom from Failure

One of the most important things wise people know is that failure is a necessary component to success. Whether one has all of the information or not, failure can happen. I've seen this play out in business when sure-thing product launches that were heavily researched failed. Take for example, New Coke, which was launched in 1985. There was nothing that new about New Coke. It tasted more like a mix between Coke Classic and Pepsi, both hugely popular sodas at the time. Coca-Cola underestimated the devotion of customers to its classic taste. Change was not wanted or accepted. Although sales of Classic Coke spiked in the ultimate show of brand loyalty, pushing sales past rival Pepsi, New Coke remained branded as a marketing blunder.

Failures don't always signify a wrong decision by a company or an individual, nor should failure deter willingness to continue taking risks. Research has shown that when you're learning a new skill, you often learn more about that skill from all the detours taken along the way than from doing it right the first time. That's not only because you're learning all the ways not to do something, but also because many of those detours teach you the right way to approach other tasks you'll need to know later.

My former consulting firm in Chicago used the same rule of thumb for all of its clients: 65% of new products and services *will* fail. I learned from them that this is a necessary path to inventing truly great ideas. Because companies typically allocate significant resources to new products and services, setting up this expectation with clients was important, especially those clients accustomed to repeated successes.

We had one client, a multi-billion dollar company, that perfectly illustrated the 65% scenario. The company's executives hired my firm to help them enter a new sector in an effort to fuel company growth. They had the technical expertise as well as the manufacturing capacity to do so. The challenge was figuring out the best way to jump into the sector and land in the white space, or blank space, where no other offering was available to the consumer. Research indicated the company had the ability to make the move, but there was no clear indication that it would work. The sector did need more effective products, but the real question was: *who* should deliver them? Our clients hoped it would be them. In the end, their entry attempt failed and their company pulled out. The important thing to know is that they turned that failure into success. They took their learning with them, and with their new understanding of what they could and could not do they re-entered an offshoot of the larger market. This time, they made a smaller-scale effort and enjoyed success.

"No matter how deep a study you make, what you really have to rely on is your own intuition and when it comes down to it, you really don't know what's going to happen until you do it.."
— Konosuke Matsushita, founder of Panasonic

Unfortunately, even though experimentation is the cornerstone of science and experimentation necessitates the likelihood of repeated failures on the way to finding answers, our society typically punishes failure. When a manager doesn't meet her numbers because she tried a new delivery approach and receives a poor review, or when a child receives a lower grade on a homework project because he tried a different (and creative) method of approaching the assignment, those people might then be less likely to take risks in the future because of the high cost of failure. If we only know a few right answers, and if wrong answers are punishable, then people of all ages learn to only regurgitate what they know for certain. That stifles creative thinking and strips people of a "can-do" attitude.

So if you fail, what do you do? I know what *not* to do: don't let it decrease your confidence. In fact, when you do fail, consider yourself one step closer to succeeding. If your long-term plan is to succeed, then the only way to stay on-plan is to learn from failures along the way. There's always some little pebble of knowledge, skill, or understanding you can find that will pay dividends in the future.

"I've come to believe that all my past failure and frustration were actually laying the foundation for the understandings that have created the new level of living I now enjoy."
— Tony Robbins

Wisdom is not about getting everything right all the time. Wisdom is about building the mental resources and emotional resilience to approach life's challenges with confidence and resolve. Wisdom is about accepting both successes and failures with gratitude for all they have to teach you.

Wise People Make Leaps of Faith

My grandfather was an idealist. Idealists have little room for reality. That can be frustrating for the rest of us because dreams need to be tethered to something tangible for us earthbound people to participate in them. However, Grandpa's idealism did make him exciting and fun to be around, because where some people don't leave enough room for imagination, Grandpa was all about imagination. And, as unrealistic as he was sometimes, Grandma and family did ground him. Perhaps his strongest tie to reality was that he was protective of his wife and daughters, and all of us.

Grandma was wise to latch onto a dreamer. She knew she had a tendency to play it safe and that her husband pulled her out of her comfort zone and helped her grow. Her life was enriched and enlivened by Grandpa's capacity to dream. Sometimes she would ask, "Jimmy, what are you doing?" or "Jimmy, have we thought of everything?" But in the end she would say, "Okay, I guess we can do it." Grandma knew she didn't need all the information, because she trusted Grandpa to take care of the imagination and she trusted herself to make the intuitive leaps of intelligent thought to fill in the blanks.

"I'll be okay because I know I'll be okay. How do I know? Because I've been through tough times and I've always been tougher than the times."
— Grandma Valentine

One of Grandpa's many dreams was to own a farm in Michigan where he could eventually move his family. In the 1940s, he bought some inexpensive land with a house standing on it that had been built more than a hundred years earlier, in the 1830s. He spent years renovating. It soon became a place where the whole family would enjoy summers while Grandpa worked on the house. He kept working on his home improvements until he was no longer physically able. I'm sure Grandma had her doubts about his dream at first, not sure if they could afford it or whether it would end up being a dream unrealized. But she put her trust in him, and as a result helped him to make his dream a reality. That old farmhouse continues to have renovation needs but it has become a beloved family inheritance that his daughters, grandchildren, and great-grandchildren continue to enjoy today.

Grandma knew that life was uncertain, whether you chase dreams or not, but she believed that if you surround yourself with people you trust, and if you trust yourself, that's as certain as it gets. She trusted herself, and she trusted Grandpa too, because even if he took risks she knew he would always put family first. Everything else was an adventure, one she might not have had without him. That was good, too. Grandma knew that not knowing wasn't a bad place to start, or even to finish.

What Would Grandma Valentine Say?

You don't need to know everything. If you understand human nature and you have confidence in yourself, that's half the battle.

A Step Toward Wisdom

Failure is one of the steps required to reach success and knowing every detail won't prevent, nor should it prevent, failure.

10

Wise People Exercise Imagination

"Imagination is more important than knowledge.
For knowledge is limited to all we now know and
understand, while imagination embraces the entire world,
and all there ever will be to know and understand."
– Albert Einstein

Imagination is the Only Path to Creation

Often when I wasn't sure what to do next, my grandma used to say, "Just use your imagination!" After that, she would become genuinely excited about the prospect of what I would come up with, and would insist on hearing all about the results.

Although I had some idea of what Grandma meant by *imagination*, it is a slippery word. We often use the word "imagination" to refer to the ability to apply different pieces of existing knowledge to create a new idea, or to picture something that we have never seen or experienced before, or to create in our mind an image of something that does not yet exist. It can be any of these things, and much more. Scientists, psychologists, and philosophers through the centuries have explored so many aspects of imagination it could take several lifetimes to examine them all.

Aristotle was perhaps the first philosopher to explore the idea of imagination, or what he called *phantasia*, and how it plays an important role in allowing people to create mental images when their senses have no input to go on. It is, in short, a form of creativity. According to Jana Noel at Montana State University, Aristotle defined *phantasia* as "our desire for the mind to mediate anything not actually present to the senses with a mental image." Another leading researcher, Jose M. Gonzalez, instructs us that contrary to many interpretations of Aristotle's *phantasia*, this concept "stands for the psychological function that mediates between sense perception and man's higher intellectual faculties."

"...imagination makes possible all our thinking about what is, what has been, and, perhaps most important, what might be."
– Nigel J.T. Thomas

Nigel J.T. Thomas is a cognitive scientist, philosopher, and historian of science and psychology who has spent much of his career studying imagination, without which he suggests we might not even be fully conscious of our own existence. Thomas studied the transformation of sensory stimulation into meaningful experience by way of using our imagination. Through this process we're able to make sense of who we are, what our relationship to the world is, what other possibilities we might face in the future, and why it all matters. Both philosophers and scientists have spent centuries pondering the connection between imagery and getting in touch with reality, connecting what our body experiences with what our mind can know. Thomas asserts that, if 2,000 years of Western thought has not dislodged the idea of understanding reality through the imagination, it's worth taking seriously.

In both the sciences and the arts, the concept of *understanding* requires the human brain to come to see some aspect of reality in a particular way. Meanwhile, the concept of *creativity* depends on coming to see things in a new way. While imagination does not always lead to creativity, all creativity does seem to spring from imagination. So, if you spend time daydreaming about the fast, flashy car you dream of buying one day, you might not produce a lot of new ideas during that time. However, if you don't allow yourself to imagine anything beyond the accepted knowledge of the past or the physical realities in front of you, then you would never produce much of anything new.

It took a leap of imagination for Einstein to theorize that space and time are relative rather than absolute, that matter could be turned into energy and vice versa, and that light moves as both a wave and a particle. Science and our world have not been the same since. He did not need to actually stare at light waves or particles to see their duality, nor could he have. He could only look at the effects they caused, and try to imagine why those effects sometimes changed. This required his brain to come up with sensory images of something *nobody had ever seen*. There's something almost mystical about that.

Imagination is not just a matter of rearranging existing knowledge into a new idea. It is greater than the sum of those parts. It requires not only adding to one's physical experiences or memories of those experiences, but also stepping outside of that to have an experience that *only takes place in one's mind.*

Because of the elusive nature of imagination, although Thomas is a cognitive scientist he finds much to value in the view of Romantic thinkers of the eighteenth century. Their predecessors often regarded consciousness as a *mirror*, which passively receives images from the external world. But the Romantics saw consciousness as a *lamp*, which actively throws beams outward into the world to illuminate experience. Thomas's studies in cognitive science have led him to support the perceptual activity theory of imagery. That is, the imagery that we process into conscious experience is influenced by the activity of our mind reaching out into the world.

As I follow Thomas's viewpoint, for me it means that imagination, or creative thinking, requires a mind that is not passive, but active. Imagination allows us to leap beyond objective reality, and to apply our subjectivity to choose what we perceive. This gives us each the exciting opportunity to change our relationship with reality. When we face problems or limitations, imagination gives us the power to invent ways to overcome them. Reality is no longer set in stone, but is an ever-shifting universe of quantum possibilities.

My grandma taught me that the mind is a muscle, so to speak, and that the more you use it, the stronger it becomes. If the imagination is as critical a component to consciousness as thousands of years of philosophers have determined, then the more you actively exercise your imagination, the stronger your consciousness becomes, and therefore the stronger your mind. Meanwhile, the more you decide to passively accept whatever comes your way without working your imagination to actively interact with the world around you, the weaker your consciousness, and therefore your mind, becomes.

People who insist on only seeing things exactly as they always have seen them, based only on information they have passively received from others, are doomed to live an unconscious life. They have limited prospects because they create nothing, and live at the mercy of what others decide to make of the world. To my way of thinking, the more you use your imagination, the more you are fully alive.

"How can anybody ever say they're bored? If they really think there's nothing to do, then they're either lazy or they have no imagination."
– Grandma Valentine

In her later years, my grandma grew concerned with the lack of active thought and, more importantly, the lack of questioning about what was going into reporting the news. In her younger years, she had seen an era of journalism that emphasized the presentation of facts. But, beginning in the early 1970s, she saw a movement that engaged reporters and news anchors to spend more time reporting not the news, but their own analysis of the news. Grandma thought this was a dangerous trend, in which news providers were doing much of the thinking for their viewers and readers instead of reporting the facts and letting people draw their own conclusions. Her key concern was that people would stop exercising their minds to analyze current events and develop their own theories of cause-and-effect. With this "spoon-feeding," as Grandma called it, she predicted that minds, as a muscle, would go limp. Grandma wanted people to use their own imaginative capabilities to create their own world views. When I watch or listen to news, opinion, or discussion programs today, I understand her concern.

Imagination and Knowledge Are a Team

Although Einstein said, "Imagination is more important than knowledge," the two do work together. If James Maxwell had not demonstrated electromagnetic theory before him, Einstein would not have taken the leap to further explain the results of Maxwell's experiments with the Theory of Special Relativity. Special relativity explains how two objects moving at constant speeds relative to each other can appear to be moving at different speeds depending on your position in space, while the laws of physics and speed of light remain the same for both of them. Part of Einstein's genius was in accepting that Maxwell's experiments and theories were correct, and then using his imagination to explain the inconsistencies between the two. So, Einstein's knowledge and imagination worked together to create something new.

Wise people recognize that the effort to apply imagination to knowledge can result in rewards that far exceed what we imagine.

I have a great respect for people who appreciate the value of receiving knowledge, and who don't dismiss it because it either seems too farfetched or too much like something they've heard before. Wise people demonstrate enough curiosity to wonder, "What new opportunity might be available in this piece of knowledge that I have not yet considered?" This type of question often opens up the creative use of knowledge and brings in imagination as its faithful companion, so that together they can inspire new ideas.

Intuition to Imagination: A Leap of Faith

My grandma and I both believed and trusted in the power of intuition. Grandma was so intuitive that she almost seemed psychic, but neither of us believed that intuition was some sort of supernatural sixth sense. Rather, I see it as the brain's ability to subconsciously process past experience, remembered knowledge, current sensory input, and imaginings about the future in greater quantities and at higher speeds than we consciously realize. To trust intuition is to trust one's own mind.

If you want to use your intuition, it's important to regularly keep the toolbox of your mind filled with every skill you can gather. Imagination is perhaps the most important tool for your intuition to grab hold of. That's because intuition requires you to remain open to ideas you can only imagine. If you doubt the validity of your imagination, it becomes difficult to act on your intuition.

When companies were laying off workers at a fast pace in the 1980s through the 1990s, my grandma and I discussed this course of events at great length. I was set to graduate from college in 1991, and I was concerned about the job market I would find myself in. The United States was in a recession. My grandma was as concerned as I was. We often discussed the economic environment and what it would mean for individuals.

As the economy contracted, Grandma grew concerned about my aunt, her younger daughter. My aunt was in her fifties, and she worked at a large business products company. The days were gone when working at a company for years was typical. My grandma often suggested to my aunt to prepare for the possibility of layoffs: sharpen her computer skills, start looking around for other prospects, and in general prepare to lose her job. At the very least, Grandma thought my aunt needed to use her imagination to develop an action plan in case the unexpected should occur. Then it happened. The company began mass layoffs, and my aunt was one of the employees cut. Because she hadn't planned ahead, she had to scramble, urgently freshening her skills so that she would be able to get another job. "In your fifties, job-hunting is much more difficult than in your twenties," lamented my aunt for years to come. My grandma did not say, "I told you so," but she continued to express concern about how it would work out.

It took a very long time, a couple of years, but my aunt finally found a job. It was not as good as her old job, but it would have to do until retirement.

Although Grandma's intuition was uncannily accurate in many instances, she did not spend a lot of time giving other people advice. She knew that my aunt, in particular, was set in her opinions about "the way things are." Although it was evident to my grandma what would happen, it was not obvious at all to my aunt. The difference? My grandma did not block her intuitive sense.

It is generally tough for people to open up their imagination to possibilities outside their experience because of the risk of letting go of their beliefs, their values, and the knowledge of reality that has served them well in life so far. But it is essential to imagine both best-case and worst-case scenarios in order to prepare the best we can for life's challenges and opportunities.

A wise person can take time processing a new idea without feeling the need to either accept or reject it. Sometimes you might even decide not to act on a new piece of information, only to discover its usefulness in some new context weeks, months, or years later. To disregard a new idea simply because, "We've never done it that way before," or "Everybody knows this other way is how it's done," or "The last time I tried something like that it turned out badly," is to risk missing important messages to the imagination. When you keep your imagination open, you keep your intuition prepared, always ready to notify your mind of all the possibilities.

"A foolish consistency is the hobgoblin of little minds, adored by little statesmen and philosophers and divines."
– Ralph Waldo Emerson

If you practice listening to your intuition, you will begin to notice that what your brain is primarily doing is ferreting out patterns in the information and experiences that come your way. Psychologists have long known that the human brain is, among other things, a pattern-recognition machine.

We look for repeating qualities in the objects and phenomena around us and try to determine the reasons behind repeating events and processes. It only makes sense that humans would have this survival skill; how else could we find food or avoid danger, unless we began to recognize the signs of food or danger? We are likely the descendants of those humans who were best at it.

Each time you recognize a pattern and are rewarded with results, either positive or negative, it reinforces your ability to recognize the pattern the next time. Soon, this sort of recognition becomes intuitive. Those of us who engage our imaginations in the process can move beyond simple sensory patterns, such as colors and shapes and smells, to recognizing the patterns in complex human relationships, social situations, and world events. Intuitive people are great at pattern recognition.

Of course it is possible to see patterns where there are none, which is one thing that causes so many conspiracy theories and superstitions to abound. But if you remain open to new ideas without feeling the need to react to or act on all of them, and if you test them using objectively measurable criteria, you can eliminate many of the mistakes that can come from allowing our beliefs or desires to influence the patterns we see.

Wisdom and Imagination Have No Boundaries

Although knowledge contributes to wisdom, they are not the same thing. My grandma strongly held this belief and would reinforce it on a regular basis. Some types of knowledge are specific, applicable only to a specific field, such as aerospace engineering, biblical theology, marine biology, real estate law, or cattle ranching. However, wisdom is so broad-based it can apply to things you wouldn't even imagine. Yes, you can apply wisdom to successfully engaging in any of the above professional fields, not just one. You can also apply it to starting a new endeavor, solving a problem with a colleague, making a big decision involving your family, training your dog, even developing inner peace or a better relationship with nature.

One human skill that allows us to apply wisdom across divergent arenas is our imagination. We observe the effects of our choices in one situation, and then we are able to imagine how it might work the next time we must make a choice. For example, my daughters might go to the park, where they have the opportunity to either play with each other and increase their sisterly bond, or add a third person and make a new friend. By the same token, I might assess the pros and cons of entering into a business partnership with someone and play all the possible outcomes in my mind. As humans, we have the capacity to run different scenarios. We can choose to combine knowledge, intuition, and imagination, but we have to be observers and learners to excel in this ability.

Once upon a time, people took more time to connect with the world around them without the use of technology, and to find metaphors in every interaction: families, leaders, communities, animals, plants, enemies, friends, waterways, mountains, the seasons, the wind, all had something to teach us. Our family has a cabin with a view of Rocky Mountain National Park. Being there is cathartic. We can decompress thanks to the beauty of nature alone: breathing the fresh air, smelling the fresh pine, hearing the rustling of trees and the activity of little birds. As I watch a bald eagle stoically perched in a tree, surveying the wild around it for miles, I remember how stillness can fill me with ultimate peacefulness.

Then, in a split second, we're driving back home so we can create other sorts of value in our respective lives as only humans know how to do. But we're also able to bring that sense of harmony back with us, inviting it into our family life at home and into our relationships with friends and colleagues in our day-to-day world. It feels worthwhile to nurture our connectedness to all living things, keeping our wisdom muscles as broad-based as possible.

In a 2011 study at the University of North Carolina at Greensboro, psychologists found that people who were higher in fluid intelligence were also significantly more skilled at generating creative metaphors for their emotional experiences. Their ability to identify abstract connections between seemingly unrelated experiences and objects was clearly connected to their ability to engage in divergent thinking when problem solving.

I believe that it stands to reason that the more experiences we are attentive to in life, the more metaphors for living we have at our disposal. In other words, the more we connect with our world, the more connections we'll find. When we increase the number of people, places, and things we connect with, this broadens our ability to take the wisdom we learn from any one of them and consider its potential application to all the others.

Did you ever know someone who had all the markings of genius, but when it came to dealing with real life that person never seemed to reach his or her potential? I believe one reason that happens is because they do not know how to make that imaginative leap that allows them to connect what they've learned in one setting to its potential application in other settings. They're stuck in specifics, and cannot imagine or intuit the possibility of making other connections and creating new patterns.

Imagination and Leadership

Can you spot a natural leader within a minute? Although there are a few ways, here's one: if I bring someone a situation and two possible solutions, option A and option B, a natural leader will say, "You might also want to consider C, or maybe D, just to see if those might give you the results you want." That's leadership. It's also clearly imagination. A leader doesn't have to know whether C or D will work, only be willing to imagine that there are options besides A and B. Leaders are able to assess situations and develop solutions that fit the strategic direction of any given situation. The important thing is opening up the playing field to more possibilities. That's when creativity and innovation have a chance to create results.

There is a good chance that option C or D will be even better than A or B. Why? Because the leader has taken the information you handed him or her, and applied the lens of intuition. A natural leader's intuition is guided by an encompassing viewpoint based on knowledge, experience, and the competitive advantage of imagination.

Imagination Forms the Foundation of Empathy

Imagination gives us the ability to see what a hypothetical scenario looks like from an emotional standpoint. That sort of imagination is called empathy. Imagination can give us answers to such qualitative questions as: What will the likely outcome be and how will it be received by those impacted? Empathy is required to imagine people's emotional reactions so we can better understand the path we decide to take.

For example, if someone decides that it will be difficult to live up to a promise made, he will run through the scenario to determine what the impact will be if he doesn't keep his promise. Empathy can help us balance the disappointment others might feel against the likelihood they'll understand our dilemma. Empathy can create guilt and cause us to stick with a promise because of the disappointment we'll create by not living up to our commitment, when the promise might not be in our best interest. On the other hand, some people block off empathy to make themselves feel better, concluding that the impact will be minimal when in fact it might not be. This is what we call rationalizing, and it is driven by intellectual activity as opposed to empathetic predictions.

Empathy is powerful. Many of the best leaders have a well-developed ability to empathize.

For wise people, empathy plays a role in making decisions that impact all areas of our lives: personal, familial or professional. For example, when a team member on a project makes a devastating decision that causes us to run a loss on a large order, what do I want the takeaway to be? Assuming I want a future relationship, I will work with that person to find ways to minimize costs, recoup the bottom line, and put processes in place to avoid this error in the future.

Empathy helps give me room to choose a course of action that will allow me to not only survive the situation, but also to empower myself and those around me. Without imagination, empathy is not possible, and without empathy the working world would be a dismal place. With empathy, we can engage in strategies that allow us to connect with other people, to turn failure into growth, and build growth into success.

Imagine Yourself Doing It and You Can

Imagination is one of the components of wisdom that allows us to create something from nothing. We can also use our imagination to inspire and motivate ourselves to success. Imagination allows us to envision ourselves doing something we have never done before, and once we envision that it becomes easier to take the steps to achieve it. Envisioning ourselves doing something new is empowering. It's a way to practice, to gain the first step of experience without the actual experience.

At my daughters' school, there was a new opportunity for parents to volunteer to teach a class. I've volunteered for my daughters' classes before and I've always enjoyed it. It's fun working with young creative minds. It gives me a sense of partnership in my children's education.

I told my daughter's teacher that I was happy to volunteer to team-teach with whomever else wanted to give it a try. That Friday when I picked up the girls at school one of their teachers said, "Oh well. We didn't get that much interest. I'm going to send out another email and see if there are any volunteers."

I said, "Whatever you'd like to do is fine with me. Even if I end up doing it by myself, I love to help out." Truth is, I knew it was a tough time of year for parents to volunteer for in-class activities.

At pick-up the next day, the teacher let me know that two other parents volunteered as well. However, one of the parents had reservations because she was not sure what to expect. The teacher introduced me to this mom, who told me she was uneasy with the idea of leading instruction for a roomful of students.

"I don't know if I can do it," she said.

"Of course you can do it!" I said. I knew she would be great because she was smart and an incredibly sweet person.

We had this conversation in front of the teacher organizing the effort when another teacher joined us. The second teacher chuckled and shared that this was going to be such a fun and memorable experience for all. We surrounded the worried mom with our attitude that there was no room for fearing mistakes. The counter to fear was making a plan, showing up with enthusiasm, and giving the students an opportunity to bring their own ideas and enthusiasm to the table. Based on my experience and the experience of these teachers, we couldn't fail.

"Don't worry," I said. "If you're doing this with me, we're definitely going to have fun. It's going to be good."

"I'm not sure…"

"Oh no, don't say that," I said. "This is going to be great!"

With continued encouragement, the other mom grew cautiously excited.

I truly believe that if I can picture myself doing something and having it turn out, then I'm halfway there. My imagination sets the stage for success. I just have to put my imagination to work at seeing the way I want things to go. I find that applying my imagination to create a positive outcome makes life a lot more fun. And things really do tend to turn out better.

We had a great time in the end. The other volunteers, the father, and the other mother were all amazing. As the early philosophers knew, where our imagination goes, our consciousness follows.

What Would Grandma Valentine Say?

It's a lot easier to get along with other people if you try to imagine yourself in their place.

A Step Toward Wisdom

You can imagine so much more than you imagine.

Wisdom's Path: Curiosity to Knowledge to Action

*"It is easy to sit up and take notice. What is difficult
is getting up and taking action."*
– Honoré de Balzac

Wisdom as a Verb

The word "wisdom" is a noun, not a verb, but to me wisdom is not real unless we act upon it. That's why I include the word "action" in my personal definition of wisdom: *the culmination of the human abilities of curiosity, compassion, knowledge, logic, and humility, used in combination to assess situations, make decisions, and take action.* My conversations with Grandma, and the evidence I've gathered from personal experience, have taught me that the path to wisdom takes many forms. However, there are signposts by which we can all identify whether we're on that path. Those signposts will repeat along the way, but generally in this order: curiosity, knowledge, experience, and action.

Curiosity about our fellow humans was the intrinsic motivation that my grandma and I had in common. Curiosity drove her to listen, observe, and study all she could about people and what makes them tick. The same is true of me, though I've pursued my curiosity into different endeavors. In turn all that listening, observing, and studying led us to knowledge. Grandma's knowledge was primarily based on experience, though she also did plenty of learning and inquiry. My knowledge has included the pursuit of a formal education, but continues to combine both study and experience. For a person who engages his curiosity in the pursuit of knowledge, experience becomes another form of research or study.

If we were to collect knowledge and experience and never act on it, it would be like inventing a cure for cancer and keeping it a secret: pointless. That might sound like a dramatic analogy unless you consider that we expect the leaders of our families, communities, and nations to use wisdom as they make decisions about everything from paying bills to levying taxes, from providing safe and healthy food to making laws that keep our streets safe, from resolving disputes to preventing or preparing for war.

The actions we take throughout our lifetime define who we become.

Wisdom is what we use to make decisions about what actions to take. Whether we're world leaders, leaders of the workplace or household, or simply leaders of our own lives, wisdom helps us make better decisions so we can take more effective action. The actions we take affect us and the people around us in so many ways we will never fully know the impact.

Inaction is just another form of action, another choice. If we want to have a positive impact on the world, then the best choice to make before any other is to employ wisdom, that is, curiosity, leading to knowledge, leading to experience, leading to thoughtful action.

When I reflect on my grandmother's actions throughout her life, I believe she would have agreed with me about this chain that leads to wise action. But although she was a complex thinker, she put things more simply. She would have said: "Use your mind. Know what you're doing. Do the right thing."

"It's easy to do the wrong thing. It takes effort to do the right thing."
– Grandma Valentine

Leveraging Human Nature

Grandma used her brain primarily in the study of human psychology, or as she would have put it, human nature. Although she enjoyed learning from books and educational magazines, her primary form of study was experience. Human nature wasn't a theory to her, but a real condition: each person has a set of wants and needs, so if you can figure out what someone's wants and needs are, you know his motivations, and when you know his motivations you can predict many of his actions and reactions. With that, you're halfway to successfully handling any challenges you face with that person. When you multiply the number of people in a situation, it multiplies the motivations, but the principle remains the same.

Using Grandma's approach, if I'm dealing with people who cannot handle standing alone and being different, then I know they'll be more motivated to pursue actions that make them feel like they belong to a group. The best way I can motivate them to cooperate with me is to figure out which aspects of our goals are mutual. Where our goals are not aligned, I appeal to their desire to belong. Personally, I'm just as motivated by solo pursuits and ideas as I am by team efforts and goals, but it pays to use my imagination when dealing with those who don't think like me, to put myself in their shoes and think about what they can get out of our interaction.

For example, when you have industries that rely on scientists and engineers to design a product, and product and marketing professionals to sell it, then you have different interests at play. I often observed this divergence of interests when I was a consultant. I once worked with a company on a challenging project to find better solutions to help people manage their weight. The team members came from different functional areas of the company and had different incentives and goals related to their respective areas. The scientists pursued options created in the laboratory, leveraging the science behind human physiology. Meanwhile, the marketing people thought in terms of step-by-step guides that would appeal to the emotions and desires of potential customers. Even though the solutions had their foundations in different viewpoints, they all provided strong potential options. Here's how we helped each group to see value in the perspective of the other: We encouraged the scientists to appreciate the psychographics of the step-by-step guides that appealed to emotion, and we helped marketing personnel understand what science revealed about the capabilities and limitations of their product ideas.

By putting myself in their shoes, I was able to recognize why one team put more of their trust into proven facts, while the other put more of their trust into the understanding of human emotions. Acknowledging the value of each helped me find the intersection between the two groups, so that I could support them in combining their efforts to find more profitable solutions. In the end, both functional areas of the company became more robust, with the marketing department appreciating the importance of not over-promising on the products, and the scientists appreciating the need to develop unique product attributes to appeal to customers' emotionally driven wants and needs.

Wisdom Seeks Messages from Experience

Making practical use of your understanding of human nature requires going beyond The Golden Rule of doing unto others as *you would have them* do unto you. Instead, it requires doing unto others as *they want* to be done unto. This brings us back to the importance of empathy in all aspects of life, from the professional, to the social, to the familial. It's critical to recognize the emotional push and pull points by which other people operate, which are not always the same ones by which you operate. What gives the other person a sense of meaning or pleasure, and how can you find mutually beneficial ways to move toward that? What is the other person's pain, fear or unmet need, and how can you find mutually beneficial ways to move away from that?

A common example is when you have to deal with a new cashier at a store who is learning to handle a problem for the first time. The fear or anxiety driving the cashier could be not knowing how to handle the situation, seeing a line build, or worrying that customers might complain. Back when I was a cashier-in-training, I learned that customers who reacted with a little humor and understanding went a long way toward helping the situation resolve more quickly and smoothly. That taught me the importance of using imagination to create empathy, and then putting that empathy to work. By recognizing my unmet need for understanding, those customers also got their own needs met more efficiently. The experience that comes with seeing and managing these situations builds and paves the way for a deeper understanding of the correlation between human emotions and human behavior.

Experience teaches people to come to each situation better prepared, but experience alone is not enough. There is a coefficient we need to use to multiply our experience, and that coefficient is the ability to interpret what experience teaches us. If you're a person who pays attention, analyzes situations, and trains herself to interpret the meaning of experiences, then you might say your experience equals x, and your interpreting skill equals a .9 coefficient. In that case, your experiences will mostly yield .9x learning, meaning you'll learn 90% of what that experience has to teach you, which is pretty high.

On the other hand, if you're the type of person who goes through life passively, not seeing experiences as opportunities but instead staying stuck in survival mode, then you might be at a .1 coefficient. In that case, your experiences are only going to yield .1x of learning. So you would only learn 10% of what your experiences have to offer. The thing is, you might survive at 10%, but at 90% you not only have a better chance of surviving, you also have a better chance of having a happy life.

In 1942, Viktor Frankl, a prominent Jewish psychiatrist and neurologist in Vienna, was imprisoned in a Nazi concentration camp with his wife and parents. When the camp was liberated three years later, most of his family had perished, but he survived. In his bestselling book, *Man's Search for Meaning*, Frankl concluded that the main difference he had observed between those who survived the camps and those who didn't came down to one thing: those who retained the resilience to survive did so by searching for and finding meaning in life, even in the direst of circumstances. You might also say that those people practiced the skill of interpreting their experiences to discover what they could learn from them.

"Ultimately, man should not ask what the meaning of his life is, but rather must recognize that it is he who is asked. In a word, each man is questioned by life; and he can only answer to life by answering for his own life; to life he can only respond by being responsible."
– Victor E. Frankl, Man's Search for Meaning

The Wisdom of the Scientific Method

To me the greatest wisdom that the modern scientific community has offered the human race is the practice of refraining from declaring something an irrefutable fact before examination. The scientific method requires scientists to disprove alternatives to a theory, thus giving more credence to the theory that survives this test. But a theory, while it may be generally accepted, is always susceptible to being disproven by the rigorous testing of a new theory. Even Einstein said that science would probably change and add to his theories of relativity in years to come, and it has. Scientists are still trying to figure out how to reconcile many apparent contradictions between Einstein's general theory of relativity and the theories of quantum mechanics. Scientific method has wisdom that takes human nature out of the picture. It only measures that which can be objectively measured, requires rigorous testing before ideas are accepted, and allows for even accepted ideas to be subject to future questioning.

On the face of it, science can seem unyielding. In actuality it requires an open mind at all times, a willingness to accept the possibility that your ideas might be wrong, even after you think you've proven all other options false. In that way, even people who have trouble with humility find humility forced upon them by the nature of the process.

A scientist remains in a constant mode of curiosity, which leads to a constant refreshing of knowledge, which leads to ever-changing action as he or she tests theory after theory by throwing things out there and seeing what sticks. That's not just wisdom in theory, but also in practice.

Passing it On Requires Patience

Just as scientists must take action to prove the wisdom of their theories, so all humans must take action to prove their wisdom—which remains only a theory until we see results. Wisdom is all about action. You cannot gain wisdom until you develop curiosity, which is a call to action. You cannot solve your curiosity until you take action to seek learning from people and sources with more knowledge than you. You cannot build on that knowledge unless you take action to gain personal experience. You cannot turn your experience into wisdom until you put that experience into action to solve new problems and create new ideas. It doesn't end there. When you find true wisdom, it is your duty to pass it on, or all that effort becomes a waste of time, just so much whistling in the wind.

Passing wisdom on requires tremendous patience. That's because you're typically passing it on to someone who doesn't know what you know, has no idea why what you're sharing is important, and may well resent the lesson because of that.

I'm a morning person. I enjoy the early hours as a time to relax over coffee, wake with the sun's first rays, and use my solitude and the clarity of mind that comes from a good night's sleep to think about what I need to accomplish. It's my time to make plans. My younger daughter is the other early bird in the family, which is a mixed blessing. On one hand, I love that we have this in common, that we can bond for a few minutes without anyone else around, and that I don't have to struggle to get her moving in the morning. We are both equally excited by what the new day has to offer and can't wait to get started.

On the other hand, if I were to give away my time of reflection every day just so my daughter and I could share our thrill over the new day, I would relinquish time I need to center myself. It's important that we each find ways to spend those early moments doing our own things. She reads, does puzzles, or paints her nails, while I write and read. That doesn't mean we sacrifice our bonding time. First thing, I hug her, talk with her for a few minutes, and focus on creating memorable moments together. Then she knows, because I've told her, "Now this is Mommy's special time. This is when I do my best thinking and planning, not only for me, but for all of us. So I need you to do whatever you need to do quietly and on your own now." This doesn't always work exactly as planned—she is after all industrious and curious—but that's okay because whatever happens, it will likely end in an opportunity to pass on my wisdom.

One day, while I was grabbing my second cup of coffee, Morgan walked across the kitchen to, theoretically, make her own toast. She was so young at the time that she could barely reach the toaster without a stepstool, but her desire to make her own toast kept her on-task. I knew she was going to have problems the moment she opened the loaf of bread. Instead of carefully opening the top and pulling out just what she needed, she used scissors to cut through both the outer plastic bag and inner cellophane and then took the whole loaf out of the bag. I leaned back on the counter, sipping my fresh, hot coffee as I watched her. I had a feeling about what was coming, so part of me wanted to jump in and help, but that would have taken away the opportunity for her to explore her own unusual approach, and I do like her to do things herself.

Here was an opportunity to teach her two things: 1) the importance of respecting other people's need for personal space, like my alone time, and 2) that people learn self-efficacy by trying to do new things on their own.

She got the slice into the toaster just fine, but then came the dawning realization, *How am I going to get this bread back in the bag?* She began making a lot of exaggerated arm and hand movements and dramatic grunts and sighs, and finally said, "Mommy, I can't get the bread back in the bag!"

"Sure you can, Morgan. Just take a moment and think about it."

She did not take the moment to think about it. The loaf seemed to grow bigger and the bag smaller, as she grew more violent with the loaf in her frustration. She stopped as if this proof of her lack of success was sure to bring me rushing to take care of everything. "Mommy, I need you to get it back in the bag for me!"

"Oh no, no. I have complete faith that you can get that bread back in the bag."

This drama went on for a holy-cow length of time.

Finally I said, "Do you understand that I have such complete faith in you that it starts out with the real simple stuff and gets really big? That I know you can get that loaf of bread back in the bag?" If she was going to make it dramatic, then I was going to make this count, to stand in for all the real drama that may enter her life one day, so that she would remember the lesson when that time came.

In response, she tried jamming it into the bag, mashing it in the process "Ohhhhh, I'm ruining the bread!"

"No, I think it's just going to be fine." Truth is, she was ruining it a little, but I wanted her to learn another piece of wisdom: not to sweat the small stuff.

She pulled it out and tried for a better aim. Part of her problem was that she allowed her frustration to stop her from seeing alternatives, such as maybe pulling the wrapper around the loaf instead of trying to aim the loaf at the wrapper. "You're so mean!" she said, near tears.

I calmly took my fourth sip of coffee. "No, I'm not mean. I have faith in you. I'm just going to go sit down and enjoy the rest of my cup of coffee."

Of course she finally got the bread in the bag. After that, she and I both knew that she would pay attention next time I pulled the bread out of the double wrapping so she could learn how to do it, that she would think it through before she pulled the bread out of the bag so she wouldn't repeat her mistakes, and that she could definitely do something new on her own even if she messed up again. She also learned that I meant what I said about not giving up my special time, because I reinforced my expectation of her being self-sufficient so I could have that time. Not a bad teaching opportunity in return for a few mashed slices of bread.

"Give a man as fish, feed him for a day.
Teach a man to fish, feed him for a lifetime"
– Lao Tzu

My grandmother always made it clear she expected me to do things for myself. Sure, when I was small she showed me how to do things, but then she stepped back and let me learn from my own mistakes and successes. She gave me advice and pointers sometimes, but at a very early point in the learning process she would say, "I think you can do that. Now go do it, okay?" This was true whether I was a girl helping her in the kitchen, a young woman applying for college, or a new professional trying to navigate corporate politics.

I've often heard parents telling their kids, "Let me do that. You don't know how," or managers telling employees, "But you don't have any experience in that department." Worse, sometimes I hear professionals telling clients, "That's not something we do," even though it is in their general area of expertise, or friends telling me, "I'd love to do that, but I don't have the talent, skill, patience, time, background"...you name it. I believe that telling other people what they can and cannot do is presumptuous. I believe that telling ourselves that we can't do something before we've even tried is defeatist. Most people are capable of more than they or others imagine.

With most goals or achievements we truly desire, it's just a matter of finding out the steps required to develop the skills we'll need, deciding if we're willing to take those steps, making a plan, and then putting the first foot forward. Although you might not have the youth to become a professional athlete, the physical and mental agility to become an astronaut, or the genius to become a nuclear physicist, there are always alternatives. Maybe you can't afford an expensive university but can work your way through a state college, maybe you're too shy to be the team leader but have the talent to be the creative director, or maybe you're terrified of learning a new skill but take it on anyway and discover you have a gift for it.

There's a reason our grandmothers told us, "You never know until you try." Because it's true. Even if you try and fail, that's only more data for next time.

"I have not failed. I've just found 10,000 ways that won't work."
— Thomas A. Edison

Curiosity to Reach Beyond Knowing

Some people think that curiosity simply means wanting to experience something for yourself, or to learn people's secrets, or to find out this or that little piece of information. Those do all fit under the definition of curiosity, but not the kind of curiosity that leads to wisdom, at least not by themselves. A bunch of disjointed facts is not knowledge but trivia, which has little use. Truly curious people try to build a store of knowledge that will help them better understand other people, life, the universe, or a specific aspect of those things in a deeper way.

Even as a child I was excited about figuring out which end was up and why people did the things they did, not just because I wanted momentary satisfaction, but also because I sensed life was big and I had better start digging now if I wanted to get to the bottom of it. I was in an information-gathering mode for many years, and will be for many years to come. I may never get to the bottom of it. But my curiosity laid the groundwork for me to have a database to tap into, which helps me make increasingly better choices and come up with increasingly useful new ideas.

Curiosity naturally leads to action. If you're not exploring information you can use, at least as a bouncing board for other things, that's a dead end. The kind of curiosity that leads to wisdom cannot be a dead end.

Often when I work with people on a new project my curiosity drives a lot of questions upfront. I can't tell you how many meetings I've been in where I've heard something that struck a chord with me and I've said something like, "Wait a minute. I want to think about that for a moment, because I sense an idea somewhere in what you're saying that might have legs."

People who know me and like to tease me, or who don't know me well enough to understand my skill at using my intuition to find useful patterns, might say, "There goes Gabrielle again, digressing."

I don't let that bother me, because if we don't take a few minutes to explore unexpected possibilities, where is the innovation going to come from? So I just laugh or push through the moment, insisting that there is value in stepping back for a moment. "Yeah, okay, I digress, but it's because I want to see if this thought could lead to something new and exciting that's worth exploring for us."

I'm also a fan of admitting, "I don't know." If I'm in the wrong group, someone might say, "Oh no! This woman has no idea what she's doing." But if I'm in the right group, that statement engenders trust, especially because I never say "I don't know" without also assuring people, "but I'm determined to find out." In the right group, admitting "I don't know" can free everyone to open up their eyes and their minds to learning new information. It changes the approach to the situation you're looking at, because you all must go back to the beginning and ask, "Okay, what do we know and what don't we know?" You start diagramming the situation. That is where creativity can begin, from that place of curiosity. It's the only place that can lead to new actions, and therefore new results.

If you pretend to know what's going on, and you say, "I think we should just go this way," and then bluff your way through it, there's no opportunity to ask questions, no opportunity to see where curiosity will take you. So you end up taking action without all the potential information.

It doesn't matter if you go through this sort of decision process with a roomful of people or all by yourself. The point is the same. If you pretend you know when you're not sure, you're already headed the wrong direction. There are too many unknowns.

For many people, financial problems start this way. Imagine a young adult looks at his or her finances and says, "I don't know where I'm going to find the next $500 I need to pay my bills this month." If this neophyte has no idea where to find another $500, but decides to pretend that this is a "Piece of cake!" then the next decision might be, "I know. I'm just going to put everything on credit." That creates a whole new problem, because if this person could not find that final $500 to pay all her bills this month, then how is he or she going to pay $500 plus interest next month? And what's going to happen if this behavior keeps up until our young friend is $5,000 in the hole and the interest is still rising? This character might have started with a simple problem that could be solved with having a garage sale or cancelling yoga classes, or calling a service provider and asking for a payment plan. If only Mr. or Ms. Piece of Cake had stopped to examine the problem and consider all the options. Pretending we have it all figured out when we don't is just asking for trouble.

Curiosity and questions precede knowledge and experience, and knowledge and experience always precede choosing the wisest possible course of action. Intuitive leaps are important too, because that's where imagination, creativity and innovation come in. But those intuitive leaps don't work alone. It's important to combine them with curiosity, knowledge, experience, and action. It takes that whole package to comprise wisdom. Wisdom is not a static thing. It requires using everything you know, everything you guess, and everything you don't yet know, all of it working together to keep you moving on a positive path forward.

What Would Grandma Valentine Say?

Nobody is interested in how smart you are. They care about how hard you work.

A Step Toward Wisdom

A robust level of curiosity is the beginning of an exciting journey through life.

Wise People Plan Goals, not Guarantees

"Learn from the past, set vivid, detailed goals for the future,
and live in the only moment of time over which you
have any control: now."
– Denis Waitley

Write It Down

There is evidence that writing down your goals will increase your chances of achieving them. A study at Dominican University surveyed 149 people from around the world, aged 23 to 72. The participants pursued a variety of goals, including completing a project, increasing income, increasing productivity, enhancing life balance, and learning a new skill. Those who wrote down their goals had a significantly higher success rate at achieving their goals than those who didn't. The participants who achieved the best results were the ones who not only wrote down their goals but also committed to specific actions, and then sent their goals, action commitments, and weekly progress reports to a friend.

Common sense tells us that being specific, making a commitment, and being accountable are critical components to achieving our potential in life. Writing it all down helps to bring all of that together. Unfortunately, most people don't write down their goals. That's too bad, because goals have an important place in the practice of wisdom, which fosters creating something out of nothing.

Goals Give Shape to Our Purpose

My grandma did not have a lot of her own goals, though I think that's one of the things that excited her about sharing her life with Grandpa. She chose to make his goals her goals, and she enjoyed having something to get passionate about. You might say that creating a strong partnership with Grandpa was her goal. She put in a lot of her own work and wisdom, sometimes more than she anticipated because Grandpa was often ill. Whatever they both put in, they were equal sharers in the results, for better or worse. Sharing the ups and downs of pursuing Grandpa's dreams bonded them more tightly as partners. Watching them work together taught me that, to some extent, goals can be more meaningful when they're a family affair.

"Always have a dream, even if it means sharing someone else's."
— Grandma Valentine

Now that I have a family of my own, I understand why Grandma placed so much importance on working toward goals, whether they were her own or someone else's. My husband,

Dylan, has driven the importance of goal-setting in our home and turned it into a family affair. I'm more than happy to participate. Every year we write down our goals and we have our girls write down theirs. We've made it into a fun tradition. We discuss and record our goals over a formal tea. As we sip tea and eat scrumptious tea sandwiches and scones, we talk about the goals we set the previous year, which ones we achieved, which ones we've made progress on, which ones we have yet to complete, and which ones didn't pan out. We congratulate ourselves on what we did that worked, discuss what we did that didn't work, and reflect on all of it. Then we share our plans on what we want to accomplish in the coming year, and discuss possible strategies and tactics for getting there.

When it comes to these family goal-setting meetings, we do our best to think big. Dylan and I establish goals that honor both the family and our individual identities. We set goals that not only excite us, but also give us an opportunity to model success for our daughters. I believe it's important for me to role-model independence for my girls, for them to see that a woman can have dreams and goals of her own apart from her husband and children. I also don't want them to ever see my happiness being dependent on what they do, and I don't want that for myself either. I have the greatest hopes for them, but Grandma's relationship with her own daughters taught me the wisdom of knowing what you can control and what you can't—especially when it comes to your children. Just because they live with you and you set the rules, doesn't mean you have all that much control over the choices they ultimately make.

Grandma and her daughters got along well partly because she did not try to push them to be like her. I know sometimes she felt that she would approach problems differently from them, but she appreciated the fact that they were loving, dependable, devoted daughters, and that was enough for her. That kind of acceptance created a peaceful feeling in the family whenever Grandma was around.

Like Grandma, I understand that my children are individuals. Although Dylan and I are teaching them foundational values, we know they'll grow into their own unique sets of beliefs, perceptions, and experiences. I want each of them to create her own existence. If I were to attach my existence to theirs, it would be like carving out a piece from each of them. They would no longer be wholly themselves. My long-term goal for my daughters is that they follow their own dreams. Although it's important to me to pass on to them the wisdom I've learned about paving practical paths to our dreams, whether they put that wisdom to work will be up to them.

For now, my dream for my daughters is that they have as beautiful a childhood as possible. When they think about me in years to come, I don't need them to think of me as the perfect mom. I only want them to think of me as a mom who had her whole heart and both feet in it.

Goals are Good for Everyone

Since Brooke and Morgan have less life experience than their father and I have, we try to guide them toward the habit of setting personal goals that combine their current interests with experiences that will provide meaning throughout their lives. We try to make sure that we all create goals that challenge us to learn new skills and achieve things we've never done before, but also don't make them so overreaching that we have trouble believing in them.

One year both girls set a goal of making the family a complete dinner. They made appetizers, a main course, and a dessert, all with minimal help. The important thing for Dylan and me as parents was giving them the opportunity to believe that they were at a point in their lives where they had grown capable of taking care of themselves and others. Of course, both girls have continued to learn more about nutrition and making meals, but it all started with the individual belief inside each of them that they could learn to do what they set out to do and then do it.

In our family, we don't always meet every goal we set, either due to unforeseen circumstances, an evolving sense of purpose, or changing desires. One year I set out to build a family wall of pictures, only to move this goal to the next year due to the time it took to compile and frame pictures. At one time or another, each one of us has had goals that either were not achieved or needed to be modified to make them more satisfying and productive.

It's important in our house to both celebrate our successes and reflect on our "misses." As we put that value into practice, my girls are discovering that there truly is learning available in *all* outcomes, whether it's the number of books they read, the number of art projects they complete, or a small business venture they launch.

Each year, as our family develops new skills, interests, and awareness, our goals shift and change. I love watching the girls as they learn that the practice of making decisions and planning goals doesn't necessarily make the process any easier the next time around. Instead, it gives them a sense of self-efficacy, the understanding that when they apply the wisdom of experience to a new situation, it won't tell them exactly where to go but will help them chart a possible path.

Although the language changes a bit, a goal-setting session for a board meeting, management team, or volunteer event planning committee isn't vastly different from a family meeting. For a company, annual goals must be tied to the strategic long-term initiatives of the organization. If you're a software company, your goals will be much different from a food distribution company. If you have a small business of 100 employees, you'll be setting different goals than a company that employs 10,000 people. Other than that, the approach to goal-setting in the workplace is not vastly different from goal-setting in one's personal life: both arenas must consider finances, talent, purpose, values, opportunities for growth, potential risks, and relative costs and benefits.

In our family, when we set goals my husband and I believe we're preparing our daughters with a skill in wisdom that will serve them for a lifetime. We're teaching them to dream, to transform those dreams into realistic goals, and to plan the steps to achieve them. And we make sure we put it all in writing.

The Bridge Between Dreams and Goals

Wisdom is not the ability to dream, nor is it the ability to achieve. Wisdom is the understanding of how to plan a path between, and then how to navigate that path's unpredictable twists and turns. Once you know where you want to go, wisdom helps you figure out how to get there, and how to recognize when you arrive. Wisdom doesn't tell me that just because I want A, all I have to do is B, and then I'll automatically get C. A wise person asks key questions about the path between those three things: Is this the best path for me? Does this path tie to my values? Is it not merely the path of least resistance, but a path that is sensible, meaningful, and ethical?

When we ask our daughters to set goals, we want them to start from a place in which they're dreaming about what can be. That takes an aspirational mindset. Aspiration by itself is not wisdom. Any fool can dream. However, without dreams wisdom doesn't have much to work with. So our dreams offer our wisdom something meaningful to sink its teeth into.

In Chapter Five, I shared my experience with the Chicago Youth Motivation Program. The YMP sent volunteers into high schools in neighborhoods with high rates of poverty and crime, where we gave motivational talks to the students. These schools had plenty of troubled, at-risk youth, so we couldn't go in without escorts. My presentations focused on the need for having your own dreams. Many of the students I talked to were kids focused on day-to-day survival, not dreams. Showing them how dreams could inspire them to achieve more than just survival was powerful. Not many of the students were used to discussing their hopes and dreams or even admitting they had any.

I had a chance to ask specific students pointed questions about their individual dreams of what they would do when they completed school. I discovered that although most were able to figure out how to get from point A to point B and survive in their current circumstances, and a few even knew that plans for the future were good to have, the majority of students lacked something critical. The one thing missing from all these kids, whether they were wise or not—was a dream. How can you set a goal if you don't want anything, if you haven't even thought about wanting anything, if you've never even considered the possibility that wanting something more was an option? Aspiring to a dream is what makes life exciting and liberating. My heart ached as I noticed this common missing piece in their lives.

You can be wise without dreams, but that wisdom won't take you anyplace new. It was hard for those at-risk youth to understand that they did not have to dismiss their dreams based on their current situation. It was hard for me to convince them that there was always a dream they could aspire to—even if they had to tailor it into a goal that fit a difficult reality. In that sense, it does take a wise person to realize, "I need to figure out what I want. Then I need to turn that into a realistic, measurable goal. Then I need to make a plan to get there."

On the other hand, I've met people of abundant means who talk plenty about their dreams but don't seem to have much wisdom to back up their fantasies. Have you ever heard a person say something like, "I really want to travel," or "I wish I could be my own boss," or "Someday I'd like to write a book," but they never seem to have a specific plan or deadline. The goal never even sounds all that specific: a nicer house, a better job, more balance in life, but no real clarity about what that means. What qualities will a nicer house have, how much will it cost, and how will you save for it? What kind of job, what kind of skills does it require, and how will you prepare to apply? What do you mean by "balance," and what will change in your life when you have it?

If someone talks about a dream often enough, you might be tempted to ask, "So, what's your plan to get that thing you say you want?"

Most people will say, "I haven't really thought about that," or they'll get irritable with you for challenging them.

Dreams are often in short supply among those who have been raised in cycles of poverty minus hope. On the flip side, wisdom is often in short supply among those dreamers who have never been taught to connect effort with reward.

Dreams are the fuel, but wisdom is the engine.
Neither will take you anywhere without the other.

My girls are learning that wisdom is what bridges the gap between dreams and goals. The head of my children's school created a brilliant project that requires all the eighth graders to write a ten-year plan as part of their graduation require-ment. Part of that plan includes their own mission and vision statements. That is to say, a declaration of who they want to be in life and what larger purpose they want to pursue. These statements can be five words or a couple of sentences. I believe it's an empowering opportunity, because when life gets difficult or downright crazy it helps to have a clear state-ment of what you value and what you're passionate about to help keep you focused on your path. When you feel alone and adrift, having a vision and a plan to fulfill it can be your best friend.

I never tell my daughters they can't do something—unless it will cause significant bodily harm to themselves or others. My older daughter, Brooke, is something of a free spirit.

She once asked me, "Mommy, can you go to college for art?"

I answered, "Yes, right after you finish your business degree."

It's not that I wanted to take the wind out of her sails. I told her that I would love it if she became an artist, but explained that she also needed to develop skills that are valued and readily used by society so that she could have a reliable way to make a living while pursuing her art as a potential way to make a living. I explained that she did not need to look at the more practical career as a Plan B or a fallback position, but rather as part of the plan to become an artist. If she ever wants to open her own art studio or art school, she'll find business skills a necessary part of running a successful operation.

I don't ever want to stop my children from dreaming. I just want them to build the reference points they need. I want them to understand that they have to connect "I want" to "how to."

In the 1990s, I became good friends with my hairdresser, who had been on welfare. She told me she believed that the TANF welfare-to-work program was the best program ever put into place by a politician.

I said, "What do you like about it?"

She said, "It forced me to come up with a plan."

She was a single mother with two small children. She explained that knowing that this welfare program was temporary, and contingent on her working her way back to a viable job, created a sense of urgency in her planning. It forced her to think about her approach carefully and to put a deadline on everything. She had to figure out what to do with her kids while she went back to school. She also had to decide what to study so she could have a career that would pay well, give her a sense of purpose to keep her motivated, give her time to spend with her kids, and help her present a good role model for them. She ended up putting herself through nursing school. Today she's a highly trained and well-paid nurse who has her own condo, successful adult children, healthy grandkids, and a joyful attitude toward life. They're not wealthy, but they have all they need, especially each other. In my mind, that's success.

Me? I always had a dream and a plan to get there. My best friend from high school used to tease me about it. On our way to the mall, we would drive by a company with my initials as its name and I would joke that it stood for the name of a corporation run by me as their CEO. "You always have a plan!" she said.

All kidding aside, I really did bolster my dreams with action, and my friend later complimented me for the wisdom in that. When we grew up, she admitted that she only teased me because she admired my tenacity. "It drove me crazy! You always knew what you were going to do with your life." I didn't always know, but I did create concrete plans and options.

Wisdom is Never Lazy

There is a component of gathering wisdom that requires the gatherer to avoid laziness. Idleness can be tempting sometimes, but the results are unsatisfying. Even if you can afford it financially, or are willing to scrape by on as little as possible, lacking a sense of purpose in life can leave a person feeling empty. My grandma always espoused the virtues of a solid working day. Our family get-togethers exemplified that value, requiring all hands to take part in the preparations.

Purpose can be derived from working toward a goal. If you want to gather the knowledge and experience necessary to develop wisdom, then you must apply curiosity to research and inquiry, step out the door to perform work and gain life experience, and spend some time reflecting on yourself and others. All of this requires time and effort.

Modern technology and transportation have made it possible for today's working class to own and enjoy luxuries that even the upper class of previous generations never dreamed possible. But modern amenities, such as TV, social media, fast food, iPods, Smartphones, and the 24-hour news cycle cannot add to the quality of our lives unless we also contribute something meaningful to society. Sadly, many people never learn this connection.

Youth apathy towards many social issues, including the economy, politics, and a range of other issues has been increasing. This lack of connection to the world around them directly ties into a lack of dreams for tomorrow. In one essay in the online Wikispaces Classroom, *The Youth's Apathy Towards Social Issues*, the author posits that youth apathy is driven by all of the time our youth spend using technology, whether it's surfing the Internet, playing video games, or finding entertainment via TV, iPods, or Smartphones. I've heard this theory shared in a variety of forums.

It's not that the lives of our youth are so easy that they can really afford to spend an enormous amount of time on entertainment. After all, they do face a shrinking job market and the rising cost of college. Still, for many young people modern life is just easy *enough* that many of them have not learned the connection between putting in extra effort today to create a competitive edge for themselves tomorrow. Many youth, especially in the United States, have no experience with delayed gratification. The promise of constant entertainment is too alluring, and it distracts our youth from forming plans for the future. Creating a dream and starting a plan to reach it from the blank slate of youthful potential requires effort, desire, and a healthy level of focused creativity.

When I worked with a consulting firm in the field of new product development, the key value we offered to our Fortune 500 clients was creating an "innovation mindset" for them. Put simply, we helped companies master the art of finding unfilled needs, or white spaces, in markets, and then filling those spaces with something people need or want. Even though it required creativity, it was a highly disciplined process. Today's educational system is not developing that kind of applied creativity in our youth.

Public schools are increasingly focused on measurable learning. The focus is not on using knowledge but on parroting facts so they can score well on standardized tests. The link between knowledge and creativity is fundamental to wisdom, because wisdom teaches us that the art of creating something from nothing is central to a meaningful life.

Meanwhile, those kids who are naturally creative are not being taught that their natural skill is useless unless it is linked to discipline, another critical component of wisdom. The wise person knows that to achieve true creativity, you need to apply discipline on the front end. The world's greatest artists have always had tremendous discipline. Few people realize that Van Gogh was more than just a tormented genius who was driven by mad inspiration into fits of perfection. He also spent hours preparing, carefully sketching what he planned to paint.

When my consulting firm identified areas of opportunities for its clients, it was part of a highly defined and measurable process that could be replicated by the client when the consulting engagement was over. The creative elements had a defined field in which to grow and measures that allowed the creators to understand if the process was going in the right direction. Creative processes need a degree of freedom to form, but they also need measures to assess their success.

Balancing Confidence and Humility

One critical component of wisdom that makes people willing to perform the seemingly dull repetition of tasks required by discipline, and at the same time fuels their creativity, is self-confidence. I'm not talking about arrogance, which is frequently created by a lack of self-confidence. When you know what you have to offer, in a realistic way, and you do the hard work required to share it, that can be a very humble act indeed.

I have tremendous self-confidence, because I've striven to acquire knowledge and because I've let experience teach me how to fill in gaps in my knowledge with intuition and innovation. So I trust myself to dream up ideas, to know which ideas have the potential for development, and to figure out the steps to get there. If I keep moving through the steps, I know I'll eventually succeed, or if I fail I'll learn enough from the failure to succeed at something else.

I know I'm not perfect. That's a second critical component goal-setters need: humility. This was my grandma's favorite quality in a person. The ability to be humble demonstrates the ability to appreciate what others have to offer. In that vein, I'm eager and willing to learn new ideas from others, and to grow. That's an important signal to send people, that you're a willing receiver of information. Without that, you're never going to get anybody to trust you enough to even begin the process of discussing opportunities.

With that combination of self-confidence and humility, I can trust myself to choose whether or not to get involved with a project. If I know my values, what I have to offer, and how to make decisions, what do I need to fear? I'm enlivened by the challenge.

The third critical component someone needs to bring to the table whenever approaching something new, in addition to self-confidence and humility, is a willingness to embark on an honest voyage of self-discovery. My conversations with Grandma about wisdom often focused on the self-discovery component, because it can be tricky. Taking an honest look at yourself can be difficult because of the complicated human brain. Emotions can play with memories and facts rather easily, and that can interfere with seeing yourself as you truly are.

If you're willing to dig deep and embrace the journey to self-knowledge, it will not only teach you what you're good at, but what you're not good at. Trying to master everything can dilute your talents. If you narrow your focus, that allows you to build on your strongest skills, becoming even more yourself. This frees you to open your mind to learn new information, listen to your intuition, and ask other experts for their help. Wisdom narrows in on the targets it knows best.

"The secret of concentration is the secret of self-discovery. You reach inside yourself to discover your personal resources, and what it takes to match them to the challenge."
— Arnold Palmer

Wise People Look for Patterns

One thing all humans have in common is that our brains are natural pattern-seekers. We're always using our senses to try to figure out how things connect. One example of this is pareidolia, the psychological phenomenon in which people look at random images and see them as significant. It's that effect that causes people to see human faces in wood grain, bunny rabbits in clouds, or the word God spelled out in an eggplant when it is sliced in half.

In psychology, pattern recognition in general refers to the process of receiving new sensory input and trying to figure out how it compares or contrasts to previous sensory input from our long-term memories. Psychology has yet to include all the specifics that go into the many ways people process patterns, but wise people understand the importance of using this skill. Wise people also recognize that others may see different patterns from them.

My grandma was a student of patterns in human behavior. She felt she could learn more about people by studying their behavior than she could by listening to what they said. She was particularly keen on this in the workplace, where people say and do things that may be driven by different needs. An employee who is vying for a promotion might have an incentive to take a different stand on an issue than a new employee who is years away from a promotion.

When you're following a path toward a goal, following your intuition is important, and one way to trigger your intuition is to look for patterns. This applies not only to looking for familiar patterns from previous experiences, but also to looking for new patterns that develop on your way to your new goal. When you pay attention to these patterns, sometimes your subconscious mind recognizes them before your conscious mind does. When that gut feeling is strong enough, I go with it. Other times, I seek more information. Even then, the patterns I see give me some idea of the kinds of information to seek.

The concept of seeking patterns is fairly simple. You recognize an old pattern that led to bad results in the past or a new pattern that makes you uncomfortable, so you change direction. Or, you recognize an old pattern that worked great before or a new pattern with a good vibe, so you keep going, confident that you're closing in on your vision.

Recognizing patterns requires practice. Each time you see a new pattern you make the best prediction you can with the information you have. Whether you're right or wrong, the experience is useful because you can file away that information. As your files grow larger, you'll become a more skilled predictor.

I remember a project I worked on with a past employer in which our team's goal was to reduce the time it took to go through the process of making a sales quote to a customer. By day, we mapped the old process versus the new process, and by night, we reviewed our notes. My job was to learn the usage patterns of people working with our old process, and to participate in group discussions to identify efficiencies. I quickly learned that it was less important to listen to the words salespeople used to describe the sales system and more important to actually watch them use the system. What was most fascinating to me was to observe the way people had to adjust their behavior to get what they needed out of the slower system. That's how my team figured out the critical components required for a better system. This way of looking at patterns harkened back to one of Grandma's important principles of wisdom: don't just listen to what people say, but watch what they do.

To the joy of our sales force, we reduced our sale quotation time from weeks to days. By recognizing patterns, we helped the company take a huge step forward toward improving the bottom line and becoming more competitive in the market-place.

No matter how good you get at recognizing and responding to patterns, there are no guarantees. The wise person understands that all paths are opportunities, and so are all results, even those that seem like failures in the moment. Wisdom is not about the achievement of success but about the pursuit of excellence, which leads us toward ever-evolving versions of ourselves and our world. The wise appreciate that opportunities for growth are available on any path. The trick to discovering those opportunities is to set a goal, choose a path, and step forward.

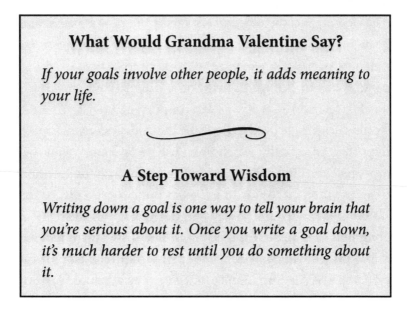

What Would Grandma Valentine Say?

If your goals involve other people, it adds meaning to your life.

A Step Toward Wisdom

Writing down a goal is one way to tell your brain that you're serious about it. Once you write a goal down, it's much harder to rest until you do something about it.

13

Appreciate What You Have

"Gratitude unlocks the fullness of life. It turns what we have into enough, and more. It turns denial into acceptance, chaos to order, confusion to clarity. It can turn a meal into a feast, a house into a home, a stranger into a friend."
– Melody Beattie

Gratitude Creates Results

Some people wait to receive the things they want in life before they express gratitude. For them, gratitude is the effect of a cause: you receive something, therefore you feel grateful. My grandmother and I agreed that this was backward thinking. For Grandma, gratitude was the *cause* of an *effect*: you feel grateful, therefore you receive. That's not to say that if you practice gratitude, your positive attitude will start attracting everything you think you want. Rather, I'm suggesting that gratitude not only makes you more receptive to what you already have, but also gives you the positive glow that attracts people to treat you with generosity, kindness, and interest. That, in turn, results in your receiving more to be grateful for.

Think of the last time you were around someone who complained about all they lacked in life. Even if it was all true, wasn't there a moment when you felt compassion-fatigue, maybe even a desire to run away and watch a Disney movie so you could remember what it's like to believe life is good? Put simply: to those of us with a sense of purpose in life, a constant complainer is a downer, an energy drain, and a magnet for trouble. Sooner or later, people tend to abandon complainers, leaving them to sit alone in the darkness they've created.

Now think of the last time you were around someone who seemed to have less than you yet who focused on all they had, or when they talked about what they lacked, saw it as an opportunity rather than cause for sorrow or alarm. Didn't you think something like, "Wow, I want more of whatever this person has"? Put simply: to those of us with a sense of purpose in life, a grateful person is an uplifter, an energy-giver, someone who makes us want to be part of his or her mission in life. Such people inspire us to bring light into the world.

"Gratitude is the *forgotten factor* in happiness research," according to psychologist Dr. Robert Emmons at the University of California, Davis. So he created the Emmons Lab, a long-term research project designed to create and disseminate scientific data on the nature of gratitude, its causes, and its implications in human well-being. In one of Emmons' studies, he had some participants keep a gratitude journal. Those subjects who recorded their gratitude tended to exercise more regularly, report fewer physical problems, feel better about their lives, and exhibit more optimism compared to those who recorded hassles or neutral life events (Emmons & McCullough, 2003).

In another of Emmons' studies, participants who kept gratitude lists were more likely to make progress toward important personal goals compared to participants who did not focus on gratitude.

In yet another Emmons study, young adults who performed daily gratitude exercises reported higher levels of alertness, enthusiasm, determination, attentiveness, and energy compared to groups that either focused on hassles or on comparing themselves with others who were worse off than them.

In yet more studies, grateful people were more likely to help others, feel relief from disease symptoms, and have more positive attitudes toward school and family.

To a wise person, Emmons' findings may seem like a no-brainer. From time to time, Oprah Winfrey has encouraged her audiences to keep a gratitude journal, suggesting they write down five things they're grateful for every day. Still, it's nice to have scientific verification, and the hope that maybe we can convince the negative people of this world that with a little diligent practice, they can actually make their lives better.

Appreciation Is an Art

Grandma and I liked to use the word appreciation rather than gratitude. Although I'm a grateful person, I believe that the word appreciation includes so much more. To me, gratitude simply indicates things you're thankful for, while appreciation has a much broader connotation. Appreciation indicates recognition of the value of something beyond its surface value, as well as an understanding of what individual things mean in relation to the whole. For example, I can be grateful to someone for sharing advice, which means I'm thankful to receive it. But when I *appreciate* that person's point of view, it not only means I'm thankful to hear it, but that I also have some sense of what it means in the big picture and that it doesn't have to apply to me for me to recognize its value.

When I appreciate the things that are right in my life, it makes it easier for me to stay strong and respond effectively when things go wrong.

I'm typically appreciative of what I have in life, even when the chips are down. But when I was younger I had not yet built up the store of experiences that have made me as resilient as I am today. I had some ability to bounce back, but I could falter a bit when negative people showed up who seemed determined to squash my bounce. I learned then how important it was to not only practice appreciation for what I had, but to also seek out appreciative people to help me through those times when it was difficult to see what there was to appreciate. For the early part of my life that person was my grandma.

When I faced difficult people who did their best to make my work unbearable, Grandma reminded me of all the positive things I received from my job and most of the people I worked with. She guided me to think of ways I could minimize negatives and maximize positives. I could avoid to whatever extent possible those people who wanted to cause trouble. I could go above and beyond the call of duty and seek to show appreciation to others who had the power to change my situation. If an opportunity arose to state my need for change, I could rise above criticizing others over personality issues, instead stating my case in terms of what I had to offer and what situations might give me a better chance to serve. In short, I could refrain from the temptation to lament problems and instead focus on demonstrating my ability to rise above challenges and perform. That's one way to show appreciation.

Grandma helped me take appreciation a step further, so that I not only showed appreciation *despite* difficult people but actually learned to appreciate the difficult people themselves. Maybe I wouldn't feel grateful for the trouble they caused me, but I could imagine what it might be like in their shoes: maybe they were unable to see past personality differences, maybe they didn't have emotional support at home, maybe they lived in fear and thought the only way they could hold onto a job was to make sure that others looked bad, or maybe their best friend just died and they weren't getting any sleep. I could appreciate that something was going on with them that I didn't know about. I could also appreciate, and maybe even be grateful for, the experience they were giving me in overcoming obstacles. That skill would come in handy.

Have you ever tried to help a two-year-old do something difficult, like climbing into a large chair or reaching a toy on a shelf, and felt the toddler's frustration? A typical two-year-old wants to enjoy the fun and accomplishment of doing things by himself or herself, and if you try to help you'll typically receive a direct and immediate response of displeasure. The kid probably won't appreciate you. Still, while it might make you hesitant to help next time, it can also remind you to appreciate that child's need for independence. Appreciation is an art because it often requires us to understand the unspoken needs of others, whether they're toddlers or not.

The Value of Intangibles

As I have previously mentioned, my grandmother grew up in the Depression era, so she was not one for throwing anything away. Not having much in her early life probably made it a little easier for her to appreciate what she did have. Her life wasn't cluttered with too many tangible items beyond what the family needed for survival: a roof over their heads, food, and serviceable clothes. The lack of physical clutter seemed to help her see more clearly the value of intangibles. Grandma could easily see under the surface of things to the human relationships and internal knowledge important to both a satisfying life and basic survival.

Think about it: relationships with family, friends, neighbors, coworkers, and employers create a sense of belonging that not only makes life more joyful but also makes it more likely you'll survive if housing, food, or clothing are in short supply. Knowledge has similar benefits, not only giving you a stronger sense of who you are but also increasing your self-reliance.

Grandma appreciated both the tangible and the intangible. She appreciated the gift of beautiful and useful objects, as well as the gifts of knowledge and human relationships. For her, remaining appreciative even when all around her appeared uncertain was the key to retaining an open mind. Saying, "I have no idea what's going to happen next, but I appreciate it," helped keep her open to discover the gifts therein.

Grandma learned the importance of "reduce, reuse, and recycle" long before it became popular. In her day that approach was necessary for survival. I remember Grandma telling me many stories about how little her family had, and how that brought them closer together. When my grandma quit school in eighth grade to help take care of her two sisters, her mother also taught her how to cook. Grandma's new kitchen responsibilities taught her another level of appreciation for food. She told me, "When we were lucky enough to have a whole fryer (chicken), we used every part. Nothing went to waste, not even the marrow." Grandma passed that lesson in appreciation on to me, along with tasty recipes that never let me forget it. She continued to make her famous chicken liver pâté well into her eighties.

As she learned to value every part of a chicken, she also learned the value of holding onto every habit and attitude her mother taught her. For her, appreciation was not just a feeling, it was an action. Every action she took until the day she died was a demonstration of appreciation.

Even during hard times, when her stomach often rumbled because the soup and coffee were watered down, Grandma found something to appreciate. She made it a point to find something to appreciate every day. She always remembered that, even if someday she had nothing else, she would always have someone around her to love. In my estimation, that power of appreciation was a skill that helped her to thrive through the Great Depression and beyond. It was a part of her wisdom that opened her to the sorts of opportunities that are always there for those who look.

"When you don't have a lot of things, you understand that family and friendship are the most important things in life."
— Grandma Valentine

The appreciation that leads to wisdom is more about life's intangibles than the tangibles. Appreciation is a value that leads not only to compassion for other people, but also to an understanding of ourselves and all we are capable of.

Count Your Blessings

The art of appreciation is often the art of valuing that which does not appear valuable: an opponent's point of view, an illness, a negative person, a loss, a criticism, a personal flaw. What if we could look at each of these things and find value?

In the book, *The Hiding Place*, John and Elizabeth Sherrill tell the story of Corrie ten Boom, a Christian from Holland who hid Jews in her home during World War II and ended up in a Nazi concentration camp with her sister. The pair ended up in one barracks with particularly awful conditions: incredibly crowded, filthy, and full of fleas. Her sister suggested that the way to deal with their horror was to follow one of the Bible's admonitions: "Give thanks in all circumstances." So they stopped and gave thanks for the fact that they had not been separated, for the realization that the crowding would allow them to share the Christian gospel of hope with more people, and even for the fleas. Corrie said she was certain that her sister was wrong about the fleas, but later she discovered that the prison guards didn't harass them as much when they were in the barracks—because of the fleas! What do we close ourselves off to when we refuse to appreciate things in our lives just because we cannot yet see the reason for them?

"It is only with the heart that one can see rightly; what is essential is invisible to the eye."
— Antoine de Saint-Exupéry

I don't believe that comparing my life to other people's, with an eye to finding my life better or worse, leads to appreciation. However, I do believe that recognizing the circumstances we share in common can lead to appreciation. The idea is not to focus on our relative positions, but on the fact that we all have trials to go through yet we also all have much to be grateful for. We are all subject to the uncertainty of the human condition. When we appreciate this, we set the cornerstone that is part of the foundation for humility.

Did you know that when Muslim people go on a hajj, or pilgrimage to their holy site of Mecca, they all dress in humble white garments? The effect is that the thousands of people gathered all look much the same, rich and poor, young and old, educated and ignorant. This practice reflects a belief that we are all ordinary humans, all born to live and die, all the same before God. The wearing of white shows an appreciation of the humanity we all share in common, and in so doing demonstrates humility. We also see this in schools that require uniforms. Stripping away visual differences allows young people to see their peers in a light similar to themselves, paving the way for shared understanding and acceptance.

Wise people do not dwell on what is difficult, wrong, or missing in their individual lives, but instead bear in mind that all humans go through ups and downs, failures and successes, love and loss. Appreciating that each of us is just one small part of a much larger dance of humanity, and that we are all in it together, can make it easier to count our blessings.

Taking Things for Granted

Humans don't just naturally come by the ability to appreciate. It's a skill. The art of appreciation requires training and practice. We have to be vigilant, to be dedicated to developing and retaining appreciation, and to passing it on to others. You only have to look at those teenagers who have been given most of life's comforts and spared most of its hardships by well-intentioned but misguided parents. The problem comes when those children are not taught the value of working for what they have. We see the results when some young people engage in lazy behavior, assuming they deserve all they have in return for simply breathing, resisting any request that they do chores, find jobs, or take interest in a wider world. Appreciation, like all of wisdom, does not just fall upon someone by chance. Parents who want their children to develop appreciation, must teach them its value.

My daughters have what they need, and my husband and I are grateful that we can provide that. However, whenever they start losing sight of what they have and act just a little spoiled in their behavior, here's what I do: I tell them, "You know what? Each one of you go upstairs and get five toys, and we're going to donate them, because clearly you have too much and you have stopped appreciating everything you have." I won't let them pick some broken-down thing either, because we're giving it to Goodwill and it has to be in good working order. It's interesting, because not only do they have to give something up, but they also have to choose what they're *willing* to give up. That requires them to think about what they have, which I hope and believe will lead to more gratitude. The lesson I'm teaching them comes from a place of love, something that my husband and I always make clear to them.

We don't only choose times when our girls are acting a little spoiled to drive home the message of appreciation. Since I believe that appreciation is a key to wise and joyful living, I find many other opportunities to help them see all they have. We do a lot of reading at our house, and I make sure the girls don't just read books about modern middle class kids, but also read both fiction and nonfiction stories about American life long ago, such as the mid-1800s. What people appreciated then is so different from what we have now. I found this particularly valuable when the Great Recession hit. I wanted my kids to understand how much Americans had to go through during earlier struggles and what they appreciated back then.

In one such book, the girls read about a character who was excited about being able to dip a piece of bread into a jar of honey, because her family couldn't typically afford such a luxury. They might have honey once in ten years. Compare that to our house, where the girls run into the kitchen, open the cupboard, and say, "Where's the honey?" fully expecting it to be there. When we talked about that story, Brooke said, "I never thought having honey was so important. It must have been hard for them. Like when I'd really like to have chocolate cake and can't have any until the next special occasion." When I hear the girls say things like that I feel my own sense of appreciation that Dylan and I are raising wise daughters who are coming to appreciate both the big and small things in life.

Appreciating the Gifts of Knowledge and Understanding

I believe the foundation for appreciation is laid when one appreciates one's own organ of appreciation: the mind. That is to say, I appreciate that I'm a living, thinking person with a brain that has the capability to consider the idea of appreciation in the first place. After that, comes appreciation for the knowledge my brain has collected from past experience, is collecting in the moment, and will collect in the future. A wise person never looks at new knowledge as a chore or burden, but appreciates that it is an opportunity to expand boundaries.

Because I appreciate knowledge, I've always had a deep appreciation for elderly people, even when I was a girl. I've long recognized a fairly basic equation: the more time someone spends on this earth, the more he or she is exposed to knowledge. Of course, that's no guarantee of absorbing that knowledge, but it does represent an increased opportunity. I show my appreciation for older people through a respectful attitude, attentive listening, and questions that demonstrate curiosity.

My mother tells me that when I used to visit our old German neighbor, Mr. Juhnke, I always put on my fanciest lace underwear and lace undershirt, as if I were going out on the town. My only mistake was that, at three years old, I had no idea that these items were underwear, not outer garments. "All you were concerned about was wearing your 'pretties,'" Mom said. Despite the misapplication, my intent was obvious to anyone who was paying attention: I understood that Mr. Juhnke was sharing his treasures of knowledge and experience with me, and in return I wanted to accord him honor and respect.

I still pay attention to my appearance when I'm meeting people I admire and respect. That's not because I believe in emphasizing the superficial, but rather because I want to offer others an external symbol of my respect, both for them and for myself. More importantly, I give them external evidence that I'm listening closely to what they say, and when I can, that I'm applying their shared wisdom to my life in a real way. Nothing gives me more pleasure than to tell a mentor, advisor, or teacher that I put to use something they taught me and that it has yielded positive results. In that way, I validate both our relationship and my growing store of knowledge.

Appreciation is the Foundation of Joy

I appreciate the American dream of pursuing our own happiness. However, I prefer the connotations of the word "joy." I feel *happy* when I eat a delicious piece of chocolate cake, but I feel joy when I feel spiritually connected to the people around me and to my own sense of purpose. My pursuit of joy is not centered on myself and what I want, but on appreciating all people and what I receive from them.

Joy is not about having what I want, but about wanting what I have. I believe that joyful living in the wisest sense does not rely on emotions that change from moment to moment, shifting according to circumstances. Joyful living is about accepting the moment as it is even if the moment doesn't precisely make me feel happy. So I can experience anger, sorrow, loneliness, betrayal, envy, fear, or any number of apparently negative emotions, and they might be appropriate to the circumstance of the moment. But there's always some part of me that remains untouched by those negatives because I feel joy in the ability to be here and experience whatever I'm experiencing. Quite simply, my joy results from the consistent practice of appreciation for the gift of life.

The sort of joy I'm talking about is immutable. I might lose work because a client shuts down her business, I might go broke, or, God forbid, I might get ill or lose someone I care about. But I would still appreciate all I have around me: the loved ones in my life and the people I have yet to meet, the life I've lived and the life I still have ahead, the existence of friends and family to help me through tough times, or the opportunity to land a new client or a new job.

What makes me a joyous person is not a specific person, job, or possession, because those things are often circumstantial. What makes me a joyous person is the realization that I am here, I am me, and I have the capacity to use my mind to keep creating ever-new circumstances and relationships for myself. What makes me joyous are the values I carry with me wherever I go, whomever I'm with.

It Could Always Be Worse

When Grandma heard someone complaining a lot, sometimes she would say to me, "They don't know that things could be worse." She wouldn't say that to *them*. She was wise enough to understand that it was not her place to dictate people's attitudes. I think it was just her way of affirming her own attitude, and reminding me of the value of appreciation.

"Everything can be taken from a man but one thing: the last of the human freedoms—to choose one's attitude in any given set of circumstances, to choose one's own way."
—Victor E. Frankl

Grandma was raised by immigrants, and their stories taught her appreciation. When she reflected on their hardships it gave her great empathy for people who were born with less freedom and opportunity than most Americans have today. She also empathized with the many poor and hungry people of modern America. Whatever people's circumstances, she believed that those who practiced appreciation were better off than those who didn't. Maybe others had lost their jobs, but Grandma thought, "At least they have their family." Maybe lost their family, but, "At least they have friends." If they had no friends, "At least they have their health." With health they could always find their way to more. Even without health, they could always find someone to love.

The way Grandma saw it, even if you lose everything, at least you have the freedom to try to make your life better. Even if you don't succeed, you still have yourself, and as long as you have that, there's hope. In fact, Grandma thought that even a person in prison could find something to appreciate, if only the fact that, though he owned nothing else, he still owned his own thoughts.

What Would Grandma Valentine Say?

"Appreciate what you have, and everyone has something to appreciate."

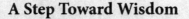

A Step Toward Wisdom

True appreciation is more than gratitude. It is understanding the value of everything around us whether we directly benefit from it or not.

14

The Wisdom of Kindness and Goodness

"Constant kindness can accomplish much. As the sun makes ice melt, kindness causes misunderstanding, mistrust, and hostility to evaporate."
– Albert Schweitzer

Benefiting the Group

For many years, great thinkers have combined the scientific ideas of Darwin's survival of the fittest, the American ideal of independence, and capitalism's ideal of competition to tell us that humans achieve the most when they pursue their own needs first. But even though competition can spur improvement and innovation, modern research has shown that compassion plays an important role in helping species survive and helping individuals thrive.

Social psychologist Sonja Lyubomirsky, a professor at the University of California, Riverside has made a career of studying happiness. Her research has consistently shown that regularly performing acts of kindness makes people happier. On the other hand, her studies have also shown that if you feel compelled to perform the same act of kindness repeatedly, it can start to feel like a chore, making you unhappy. But that seems to simply indicate that it's also important to be kind to ourselves and to not let ourselves become depleted by doing for others. This self-care may, in turn, keep us energized to continue giving.

A couple of Lyubomirsky's recent studies have shown that kindness benefits us in many more ways than simply making us feel good. In one study, children were asked to perform acts of kindness over several weeks. Not only did they report feeling happier, but they also became more popular among their peers. More people liked them. Meanwhile, at a company in Spain, she asked people to be generous to a random list of colleagues, which produced increased happiness not only for the givers, but also for the receivers and the observers. That's right: even people who simply *witnessed* other people performing acts of kindness felt happier as a result and were more likely to pay it forward by acting more generously themselves. By being kind, we actually create a happier world around us.

Social psychologist Jonathan Haidt looks at kindness as part of the overarching idea of doing things that benefit a group. This includes performing acts of self-sacrifice. According to Haidt, the benefit the group receives isn't as much from the altruistic acts themselves as it is from the increased sense of "groupishness" which altruism creates. This "groupishness" relies on values that contribute to group success.

In his book, *The Righteous Mind*, Haidt argues that natural selection is not just about individuals competing with other individuals, but also about groups competing with other groups. Both result in survival of the fittest, but what makes one group more "fit for survival" than another appears to largely depend on which group is internally cohesive, cooperative, and altruistic. Years of research have led Haidt to conclude that humans build communities from sets of shared moral values, and that they'll fight and even die to defend those moral communities.

His experiments have found six primary sources for human moral values. They are:

1. *Care* for others/Protecting others from *harm*

2. Treating others with *fairness*/Refraining from *cheating*

3. Defending people's *liberty*/Protecting against *oppression*

4. Honoring *loyalty*/Rejecting *betrayal*

5. Respecting legitimate *authority*/Rejecting *subversion*

6. Honoring the *sanctity* of traditions and ideals/ Not engaging in *degradation* of a group's traditions and ideals.

Haidt believes that one reason Americans from different political persuasions are at such odds is because they emphasize parts of these six moral codes in different ways, with conservatives believing that all six sources have equal weight and liberals believing that the first two, care and fairness, deserve more weight.

Haidt believes that if we open our minds to this realization, and find ways to see each other as part of the same group, we can begin to close the gaps in some of our differences. He was a liberal when he started writing his book, and says he has become more conservative since, though he now sees value in both. He believes one simple way to get Republicans and Democrats to set aside partisanship in favor of cooperation is to turn back the clock to the time before Gingrich told Congress, "Don't move to Washington." Prior to that, politicians on both sides of the aisle spent more time in the same town, getting to know each other, becoming friends, becoming part of a cohesive group. He believes Congress would benefit from being more groupish, but groupish as *one* unit instead of *two*.

My grandma would have simply said that we need to develop compassion for people who don't share our views and be willing to listen to each other with civility and respect, assuming the best intentions. This, to me, is another way of saying, be kind to one another. Kindness is another form of wisdom in action.

"And be kind to one another, tenderhearted, forgiving one another, even as God in Christ forgave you."
– The Apostle Paul (Ephesians 4:32)

Kindness Requires Hard Work

Human nature suggests that it's easier for people to hate each other than to love each other. When we're uncertain about others and their intentions, we resort to primitive survival instincts, feeling mistrustful of strangers, declaring people who are different our enemies, and resorting to violence to solve disputes and defend ourselves. The only way to overcome these knee-jerk responses is to gather information, ask questions, and gain firsthand experience. We must open ourselves to the possibility that someone we don't yet know might have something valuable to offer us or our group. This means accepting a reasonable amount of risk. In other words, overcoming our primitive defensive instincts requires us to engage in mental, emotional, physical, and even spiritual work. It calls upon us to risk being vulnerable to others by showing them care, interest, and respect.

"Being kind takes work. You always want to find the energy to be kind."
— Grandma Valentine

Many life experiences have taught me the power of kindness in transforming people and situations. No matter the endeavor, so long as people are involved, emotions are sewn throughout the issues that arise.

Emotions often become heightened when dealing with one of the most precious priorities in people's lives: their children. I've spent the past nine years working as a volunteer for a variety of school-based teams, events, and initiatives at two different schools. As such, I have come into contact with a wide variety of parents and educators, all of whom want what's best for the children, but many of whom have different ideas about how to achieve that. At our school, "be kind" is our one rule. For me, finding the energy to be kind one hundred percent of the time is the key to success in all aspects of any school system. We still hold everyone in the school community accountable for their behavior, children and adults both. Balancing kindness and accountability is not always easy, but we find it's the best way to function effectively as a group.

Sometimes I've been surprised to see the occasional parent react harshly when someone at the school disappoints his or her expectations. Regardless of whether I agree or not with a parent's position about what is or isn't being done for the children, I know that if I engage with her at the same level, we might find ourselves in a battle, either against each other or with each other against another person—and that will never work. Instead, my fallback position is to take a deep breath and use my compassion. I remind myself how easy it is to lose perspective when what is most precious to us is at stake. I tell myself, and her, that we both have the best interests of children at heart. When I voice interest in her position, truly listen, and do my best to understand, while also setting a boundary that requires us to address each other with respect, this gives both of us a better footing. I accept the possibility that the other person might be right, or I'm at least willing to let her be wrong without feeling the need to point it out.

When I react with kindness to the anxiety, anger, or frustration of a student, parent, teacher, or administrator, it creates a space to discover that opposing views are not as far apart as we think and compromise is often possible. When we remember that we all have the same priority, the children, many find it easier to return to kindness. That value of kindness strengthens the sense of groupishness that Haidt proposes is so important to human survival and success.

Our egos rarely embrace treating someone else's needs and desires as if they're as important as ours. But if we're wise, we tuck the ego away in a mental corner, or ask it to serve our long-term goal of positive networking for the good of the group. The hardest part is that we can't fake it. If we're phony, intuitive people will detect it. We must reach for the part of ourselves that truly can imagine walking in another person's shoes, even if we would never in a million years willingly put on those shoes. People who do this best often become leaders in a group.

You have to think to be nice. You don't have to think to be mean.

To be nice, it helps to understand what triggers other people to not be nice. At the most basic level, they simply aren't using their higher-order thinking. But why? Maybe they're tired, or hungry, or have had a bad experience in the past that colors the way they see the current situation. Maybe it's simply not a priority for them and therefore they lack the ability or desire to recognize other viewpoints. Or maybe it's psychological, an actual mental or emotional disability beyond their control. Wise people prioritize the role of kindness in creating a better world for all of us. Encouraging everyone to embrace that priority is an ongoing challenge for the human race.

Being Good to Yourself Doesn't Mean Self-indulgence

Kindness is a time-honored human tradition. It is a core teaching of many religious theologies and spiritual practices.

Whatever our beliefs, emotionally healthy humans all value kindness.

According to Christian tradition, Jesus advised his followers, "Come, you blessed of My Father, inherit the kingdom prepared for you from the foundation of the world: for I was hungry and you gave Me food; I was thirsty and you gave Me drink; I was a stranger and you took Me in; I was naked and you clothed Me; I was sick and you visited Me; I was in prison and you came to Me" (Matthew 25:34 – 36). Jesus went on to explain that performing such kindnesses for anyone was the same as performing them for God, "...inasmuch as you did *it* to one of the least of these My brethren, you did *it* to Me" (Matthew 25:40).

According to Buddhist tradition, Gautama Buddha suggested, "Teach this triple truth to all: A generous heart, kind speech, and a life of service and compassion are the things which renew humanity."

According to Islamic tradition, the prophet Muhammad said, "Be kind, for whenever kindness becomes part of something, it beautifies it. Whenever it is taken from something, it leaves it tarnished."

Religions and modern psychological theories also tout the idea that it's important to not only love others as much as we love ourselves, but to do the converse: to love ourselves as much as we love others. According to Buddha, "You, yourself, as much as anybody in the entire universe, deserve your love and affection."

According to the Jewish Torah, "He that getteth wisdom loveth his own soul: he that keepeth understanding shall find good."

The Hindu Bhagavad Gita makes it clear that loving yourself is not about being selfish, but has a much higher purpose: "This self-pity and self-indulgence is unbecoming of the Great Soul that you are."

Taoists meanwhile, believe that goodness can perpetuate amazing changes, but that all goodness begins by first demonstrating goodness to oneself.

When you demonstrate goodness to yourself, it gives you the positive energy to demonstrate goodness in your community, where that positive energy passes on to other people who then feel inspired to also behave with kindness. This chain reaction exponentially spreads the power of each generous act. This practice of being kind to yourself might sound easier than kindness to others. But wisdom teaches us that being kind to yourself requires as much thought as being kind to someone else, or more.

Does being good to myself mean indulging myself in whatever gives me pleasure, such as spending a day pampering myself at a salon, going on a shopping spree, or ditching work and playing hooky at the movies? It seems to me that being kind to ourselves is more about committing to ourselves, believing in ourselves, and trusting in ourselves. It means giving ourselves the opportunity to become the best version of ourselves, doing the hard work required to achieve that, and trusting ourselves to succeed. It means pursuing our dreams, hopes, and aspirations as if they matter. It means finding a purpose in life and fulfilling it.

Our greatest aspirations often involve becoming part of something greater than ourselves, so we can give something back: maybe to another person, to our community, to the environment, or to the world. So you might say that, while kindness to ourselves gives us energy to be kind to others, being kind to others is often the very path to being kind to ourselves. By giving ourselves the fulfillment that kindness to others offers, we are giving ourselves a gift.

I believe the greatest acts of kindness we give to ourselves and to others are not tangible. Sometimes intangible gifts require the greatest effort. For example, it's not easy, but I always do my best to give myself the benefit of the doubt, to have confidence in myself, and to believe in my own goodness. I try to be good to myself via the simple things, such as eating healthy food and getting enough sleep, as well as via the more idealistic things, such as not beating myself up for making mistakes. I sometimes give myself the gift of correcting or making amends for my mistakes where I can, learning from them so I won't repeat them, and doing better next time.

I believe one of the greatest acts of kindness we can offer ourselves is to accept ourselves as human, capable of creating great things, but also subject to limitations. My grandma would simply have said, "How can you give other people understanding unless you give yourself understanding?" It's the gift that keeps on giving, because once we give it to ourselves, it's easier to pass it on.

"Love yourself first and everything else falls into line.
You really have to love yourself to get anything
done in this world."
— Lucille Ball

Love isn't a Test

It was Grandma who constantly reminded me to learn from my mistakes, forgive myself, and move on. That practice brought me so much relief that I wanted to share the gift with others: to accept their mistakes, forgive them, and move on. That kind of love takes a lot of energy. It means you cannot keep your thoughts to yourself.

When you see sharing understanding, kindness, and compassion as one of your missions in life, it also requires making yourself vulnerable. The problem is that many people are afraid of being vulnerable, so they will throw a lot of junk at you to make you prove your love before they'll trust it. People constantly test love, but they rarely test hate. It sounds counterintuitive doesn't it? You'd think it would be the other way around. But there it is. When people sense that another person hates them, they tend not to push that person's buttons, because they'd rather avoid the confrontation and they know there's no percentage in it. But if someone knows you love him, especially family, and most especially children, he'll push every button to see if he can make you dance. My theory is that if we did this less, we would have a lower divorce rate and fewer family squabbles in America.

Those of us who work at wisdom work hard not to test the people we love, and teach our children to avoid it too. We try to see love as a gift, and to return that gift with kindness. During twelve years of marriage, I've learned where Dylan's hot buttons are, and as a gift of love to him I do my best not to push them. In return, he does the same for me. Why would I risk a happy marriage on spending every waking moment forcing my husband to jump through hoops to prove he loves me? That wouldn't be love but more like a battle. It's true, sometimes he can't fulfill my every need, but I can't fulfill his every need either. As adults, we've learned to fulfill some of our needs elsewhere—at work, with friends, with other family members, or within ourselves. If we don't get everything we want in our relationships, we try to be grateful for what we do have and let go of the rest. Love is a gift, not a test.

Dylan and I also encourage our children to avoid pushing those hot buttons, not only other people's buttons, but also their own. It's one of our family values to stay positive, especially when it's tough. In fact, we've created a family mission statement in which we've declared that none of us will use the word "can't" when we talk about abilities, whether our own or each other's. I believe that's one reason the majority of our family life is peaceful, productive, and mutually supportive.

Although kindness begins at home, wisdom dictates that it doesn't end there. The more I've learned about my own shortcomings, the more I've learned compassion for the shortcomings of others. I've experienced first-hand the pain of failure, so I empathize with what other people go through when they fail. Whatever struggles I've been through in my own life make me want to help make life easier for others. Grandma was good at paying attention to other people, learning their gifts, and encouraging them to pursue those gifts. Through our conversations she figured out early on that I had a big heart for other people, and she encouraged me to grow into that.

Grandma loved the fact that I volunteered much of my spare time after graduating college. I helped raise money for United Way, worked at the Anti-Cruelty Society of Chicago helping reunite owners with their lost pets, and spoke to at-risk youth at high schools.

Grandma always started our phone conversations with, "So, what is Gabrielle up to now?" She knew I still had the same job, so I knew this question was meant to inquire about how I was helping other people.

The reply often went something like this, "I started the week organizing names for soliciting donations. Did you know that United Way supports hundreds of organizations that help people in a variety of ways? I think it's one of the most efficient ways to give money, Grandma. A twenty-dollar donation can go where it's needed without me having to figure it out." If it sounded like I was pitching her, it was because I believed in what I was doing, and she knew that.

So she would reply, "Keep doing all of these wonderful things, Gabrielle. It's so important to help other people. You're doing good work." That sort of acknowledgment was one of her kindnesses toward me, and I still carry it with me everywhere I go.

Kindness Finishes First

You may recall my story of a tyrant I had to work for and how my grandmother advised me to not burn bridges with my employer. I still defended myself from his negative attacks and spoke up for my coworkers in a respectful tone. But I avoided taking on the position of a whistleblower, which at that stage of my career would only have earned me a reputation as a troublemaker. Just to underline why kindness is so critical to one's survival, I'd like to share with you how that story turned out:

After ten years, I left that company with my reputation intact. Meanwhile, the boss who had made my life miserable stayed there for several years. According to one of my colleagues, he did not change his ways. It's always disappointing when time does not teach unkind people the value of changing their ways. Kindness was never a priority for him, and there was no evidence it ever would be. He was eventually asked to leave the organization, and I was led to believe it was due to his "management style."

The most important lesson I learned from that situation had little to do with my difficult boss. Rather, the lesson I held onto came from my grandma. She not only offered me her advice, but she did so with the greatest of kindness. She knew that her best advice was going to be tough for me to hear, and her empathy made it possible for me to listen because the kindness shone through. She made it clear that she understood what I was going through, and she agreed it was a tough situation to endure. She also made it clear that when she told me to keep my head low, she was trying to save me from even worse pain and potentially long-term negative consequences to my reputation and career. Most importantly, she told me the truth with a quiet voice, a gentle attitude, and a calm confidence.

Grandma showed me by example how to get people to listen to reason, and she did it gently: "You know if you lose your temper and confront him too boldly, it's not going to be good for you."

When he took himself down years later, without my help, I saw the results of her wisdom. She was no longer around, but I'm sure she knew what I would have told her: "You were right, Grandma."

Kindness doesn't always look the way we think it will. Grandma's kindness was to tell me what I needed to hear even though I didn't want to hear it. Sometimes we show someone love by being the person she can count on for the truth. Sometimes we show kindness by telling her she has spinach in her teeth. Kindness is at its most selfless when we genuinely care more about helping someone else be her best than we do about impressing her. With kindness, as with any gift, it's the thought that counts.

What Would Grandma Valentine Say?

You can't help anybody until you first try to see things from their point of view.

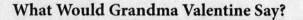

A Step Toward Wisdom

Some wisdom can only be understood by those with the kindest of hearts.

Truth and Decorum

"(George) Washington's entire honesty of mind and his
fearless look into the face of all facts are qualities which
can never go out of fashion and which we should
all do well to imitate."
– Henry Cabot Lodge

The Effectiveness of Honesty

It's easy to believe that nice guys finish last. Individuals behind the mortgage crisis during the early 21st century have gone unpunished for permitting careless lending policies, even though corporate entities have been fined and received more regulations. Can a corporation make bad decisions or is it really the individuals within the corporation? Throughout history, oppressive groups and radicals have snuck into the power voids created in the wake of hopeful young revolutionaries overturning old dictatorships. Modern politicians regularly rise from the ashes of corruption scandals to win again. So where is the wisdom in being wise?

There are many ways to measure success, but hoarding money or power has little to do with a sense of purpose or meaning, of self-confidence or satisfaction. If we try to obtain money or power by lying, cheating, or avoiding accountability, we lose a piece of ourselves. We may become successful, but our true selves will no longer be around to enjoy it.

Honesty is the path to the kind of success that leads to peace within. If you're thinking, "But you can't eat 'peace within,'" you'll be glad to know there's more to it than that. Research shows that honesty also yields measurable external results.

In 2012, psychologists from the University of Notre Dame conducted a study on the "Science of Honesty," which showed that people who reduced the amount of lying they did enjoyed improvements in both their physical and mental health. Study authors Anita Kelly and Lijuan Wang conducted their honesty experiment over ten weeks, with a sample of 110 people ranging in age from 18 to 71 years, with an average age of 31. They instructed half the participants to stop telling both major and minor lies for the duration of the study. The other half received no special instructions. Both groups came to the lab weekly to complete health and relationship measures, and to take a polygraph test assessing the number of lies they told that week. According to Kelly, Americans average about eleven lies per week.

Over the course of ten weeks, the participants who told fewer lies experienced significantly better health. When participants in the no-lie group were successful at telling three fewer white lies a week, they averaged about four fewer mental-health complaints, such as feeling tense or melancholy, and about three fewer physical complaints, such as sore throats or headaches. Meanwhile, when control group members told three fewer white lies, they experienced approximately two fewer mental-health complaints and one less physical complaint.

The participants in the no-lie group also reported markedly improved personal relationships and social interactions.

The pattern was similar for major lies.

It stands to reason that improved social interactions can improve one's chances at creating the positive social networks that also improve one's chances of garnering success. In any case, life usually feels better when our health, mental well-being, and relationships are all in working order. According to the Notre Dame study, honesty is the path to a more satisfying life. To me, honesty is the wisest policy for the most profound sort of success.

Lead By Example

Honesty is a much bigger idea than simply refraining from lying. It's about discovering who we are and what we value, living in line with that, and being accountable for our words and deeds. If you're honest, the thing that probably frustrates you now and then is not the work that you put into living honestly, but rather all the people you run into who don't bother with honesty and accountability in their dealings with you. While we can't control the behavior of other people, we can influence it. I'm a big believer in one of the simplest things my grandmother showed me, which your grandmother likely showed you: lead by example.

Telling people, "It's important to me that you be honest with me," does not carry much weight with someone who figures that what you don't know won't hurt you. By the same token, telling people, "I promise to be honest with you," doesn't carry weight with someone who believes you might simply be the type of liar who doesn't caught. But if you live with a profound commitment to being straight with people about who you are and what you do, and to being accountable for your word, over time people will discover they can count on you. The more they see the positive results of that kind of relationship, the more likely they are to engage in the same behavior—if only because they see how many more people they can win to their corner.

"Lead by example" is a favorite saying of my husband, Dylan. To him, it's a keystone to rearing wise, thoughtful, caring young ladies. It takes a lot of patience because the girls don't instantly see the results. They have to observe for themselves over time the positive relationship their dad creates with them and with others through his honesty and accountability, and learn for themselves over time the negative results that accrue when they don't follow the same policy. This isn't only true with kids, but also with friends, colleagues, employees, neighbors, and all the people we have to relate to on a regular basis. When people see that you're honest with them, and that you reward their honesty with you, they're more likely to tend in that direction in their dealings with you—and with others.

"If you always tell the truth and do your best, good people will learn to value you."
— Grandma Valentine

Honesty and leading by example go hand-in-hand, because if you're not true to what you value, how can you lead the way to those values? The Father of Our Country understood that honesty was the founding principle of leading by example. Before George Washington became president, he was a general, and as a military leader he was known as a man who would never ask his men to do anything he wouldn't do. He even went so far as to go unpaid for his services, because he didn't want there to be any confusion about his belief in what he was doing and his respect for the sacrifices of his men. In that way, he was not only true to himself but also to everyone under his command. He proved there's a lot more to deep honesty than simply admitting you chopped down a cherry tree. Establishing the habit of honesty is valuable in practicing intellectual honesty, without which wisdom cannot exist.

Keep it Real

My daughters were both invited to apply to the National Elementary Honor Society, and they very much wanted to be accepted. The application asked for an intense amount of information, partly because it's also aimed at older kids who tend to participate in a more complicated range of activities. While Dylan and I believe in giving our girls a well-rounded education, complete with extracurricular activities, we also believe it's critical not to over-schedule them at a young age. We want them to experience the importance of playtime, family time, and downtime. But when they weren't able to fill every line on their applications they grew upset and anxious, worried that somehow their National Elementary Honor Society applications would not measure up since they didn't have an unusually high number of activities. I saw this as a teachable moment, an opportunity to let them know that being themselves was more important than trying to fill up a list of categories.

I basically said, "What you do fill in, you have to believe in. It has to be something that is genuinely an important part of your life and interests. You don't have to have 100% of the application filled from top to bottom."

But they were stuck in their fear. "If we don't have it all filled in, they're going to mark it incomplete. We won't be good enough and we won't get in! Other kids will have theirs completely filled, and we're going to be rejected! We need to do some more activities or think of more stuff to say." They said this in concert, as if this had been a repeated conversation with their peers who were also eagerly applying.

"It's not *how much* you do that's important. It's *what* you do." I followed that up with a few more thoughts regarding the application process from my earlier learnings: "What you have done here is you. Finding more things to say that aren't really important but you present them as such is not presenting the *real* you. If you did that, you wouldn't get in based on who you are. We're not going to do more stuff, and we're not going to arbitrarily add stuff to fill a form. Just put yourself out there, just you, the way you really are. They know you're eight. They know you're ten. They know you don't have as much life experience as a thirteen-year-old because you haven't been around as long."

They still weren't convinced, but I held the line in the face of their emotional onslaught, knowing that in the long run this value would sink in as they discovered the rewards of truth. Bottom line: they both got in, despite their panic over having fewer activities. How did they impress the selection

committee? I don't know, but I can guess: they took on meaningful leadership roles that came to them, which is plenty impressive for two elementary school kids; and in their essays
about why they wanted to be members, it was clear that their
interest was genuine and their commitment solid.

A lot of adults can use the same lesson. We often hear
about adults who are over-scheduled and cannot keep up with
their commitments. Or worse, they pad their resumes. There
are too many ways that can backfire. If you get caught, you're
forever the person who lied on her resume. There are a lot of
people in this world who have intimidating credentials, and
it can make the rest of us feel pressured to make our lists just
as jam-packed, but people who understand how leadership
works know that quality and focus are more important than
quantity.

It is possible to do too much, to be spread too thin, and
have people wondering, "Doesn't this person have a life?" Isn't
having a life part of what puts a leader in touch with ideas and
solutions for the real world? When we seek people to work
with and associate with, all we really need to know is that they
have a genuine commitment to those skills and values we're
looking for. More than that can raise the question: is this
person for real?

---

*Trying to be all things to all people is exhausting,
and sooner or later they'll find out you're not all those things.
Just be yourself, and like-minded people will show up.*

Some people believe that any venture involving more than one person is likely to involve game playing. If so, would that be dishonest? It depends on what game you're playing. If you play by a set of rules that's moral and honest, in keeping with your values, there's nothing wrong with playing some of the so-called games of the social, political, or business worlds. The word "game" can mean something fun we do with others that has rules of play, or it can mean a system of manipulations we enter with the intent of winning at the expense of others. If you end up in a situation that involves the latter game, what do you do? Honesty does not necessarily mean you refuse to enter the arena. Rather, you find a way to remain true to yourself and what you value despite what other people are doing.

During my tenure in corporate America, I had a few wonderful bosses. Before I left the corporation I had been with for ten years, my last boss was one of them. He was from accounting, I was from marketing, and together we worked in logistics. I had tremendous respect for him, and I believe he felt the same about me.

Still, I surprised him a bit when he told me it was time for my first review with him as my superior and I said, "I don't need to have a review."

He looked a little puzzled and said something like, "But it's time for your review. Why don't you just come and sit down in my office. It'll be fine."

Not wanting to be disagreeable, I said, "Oh gosh, all right." I followed him into his office and sat down.

"Do you want the long version or the short version?" he asked.

"Short, please, because this really isn't necessary." My tone was friendly and respectful, but also made it clear I was telling the truth.

"I can't believe it. You don't want this?"

"No," I said. "At the end of the day, you're only allowed to give me a rating between 'meets expectations' and 'potentially meets expectations.' I can never be rated 'exceeds expectations,' because then you'd have to give me a raise commensurate with 'exceeds expectations,' and you don't have that money in your budget. I already know you're only prepared to give me a raise that correlates with 'meets expectations.' So everything in my review, regardless of how I performed, is going to be a 'meets expectations.'" I explained that we had great day-to-day communication, so I already knew what I was doing well and what I could do better.

He had to laugh. He and I both knew that most ambitious young employees would come in and say, "Oh yes! Please! I want to hear all your input about how great I am and how I can be better!" That's because most young people assume they're going to be rated on how they actually performed. I knew that the evaluation had to be in line with staying on budget, and he knew I was right. This isn't true in every organization, but I'd been at this company for ten years and I knew the drill.

My colleague appreciated my candor, but he still had to go through the process. So he ran through the ratings quickly, smiling at some of them. He would tell me how I'd done in one area and I'd happily say, "Okay. Next."

He chuckled and said, "Okay, I'm only going to say a few words here, so don't rush me."

In our case, even though we both acknowledged that a game was being played, there was nothing dishonest about it.

In fact, it became another opportunity to demonstrate our honesty and mutual respect, and to even engage in some playful bonding.

My grandma taught me that decorum does not have to leave the room just so a person can be honest. She said it might take more effort to find a polite way to speak the truth, but that it is worth the trouble. To her, demonstrating good manners was just as important as honesty when you wanted to show someone respect. The two ideals don't operate in isolation.

Accountability

Honesty has a before and after. The *before* is your words and actions, and the *after* is accountability. So you could say that accountability is the last word on honesty. I believe that accountability is the flip side of entitlement, and we must, must, must teach it to our children. Here's how that works at my house:

I found out at one point that Morgan was doing her homework but failing to turn it in. Missing that crucial final step was killing her grades. She received high grades on her tests in math class and on whatever homework she remembered to turn in. But she did not think about what would happen if she forgot to turn in her work. I told her that there would be consequences for tardy homework, but she allowed herself to get distracted. She couldn't immediately imagine the consequences that might result if she continued to miss turning in her completed work. Then one day we looked at her midterm report card online, and accountability hit her like a brick.

"Oh, look at that," I said calmly, but pointedly. "You're now at a B. You're at 87. Morgan, look at your grades. Look at the impact of that homework that wasn't turned in. Look at that test that wasn't signed and turned in."

She's an engaged, academic-minded student, and she was stunned. "I got a B? But I do all my homework and I do all the work and I always get A's."

"Right. But if you don't turn it in, it impacts your grade." Here's where I made the accountability clear: *"You've got to fix that."*

Some parents who know that their kids do well in school and have done the work might be tempted to say, "I'll talk to your teacher and straighten this out because you should get credit for what you did." Some people might think, "But she's only nine." That's a good point. She is only nine. That's why I don't expect her to never make a mistake. However, just because the snafu is an understandable childhood mistake, that doesn't mean it's something I should overlook as a parent. Quite the contrary. That's the perfect time to teach her that she's accountable for her behavior. If I smooth the way for her now, how is she ever going to learn to correct her course? If she doesn't learn how to fix her own problems now—under her parents' guidance—then what will the rude awakening be like when she's an adult and she gets fired because she did all the work but simply failed to submit it?

So I didn't try to make it all better. Instead I pointed at her grades and said, "That's too bad." Then, to make it clear that I really did understand how important the National Elementary Honor Society was to her, I added, "That Honor Society looks at you every semester. So even though you got the invitation to join and be a member, you have to work on staying in and making the grade average requirements."

Do you know what she did? She started turning her homework in.

"It is wrong and immoral to seek to escape the consequences of one's acts."
— Mahatma Gandhi

A wise person knows that if you are not accountable for your actions, it can cause people to lose confidence in you. In turn, it makes them less likely to want to be there for you. If people find out that they can't rely on you to do what you say you're going to do, how can you rely on them? What's their incentive for being honest and real with you if it's not reciprocated?

In the news, we regularly hear stories about politicians trying to sidestep the consequences of corruption. They say they're in it for us, but we often find out they're in it for the money, the favors, and the power. When that happens, our representative system begins to break down. When society loses trust in its leaders, it becomes easier to think there's no point in being trustworthy ourselves. If we want our lives to get better, we cannot simply point our fingers and say, "Everyone else is doing it."

There's only one person you can be accountable for. Yourself. It is when you decide to take responsibility, even when the world tempts you to think it's not important, that you show your wisdom. Change starts with individuals, individuals who lead by example.

Walking the Talk

My grandma sometimes said of politicians, "I don't even listen to their words because seldom do their words reflect the actions they're taking." She knew that the only way to see if they were true leaders was by waiting to see if their actions matched their words. She wasn't only looking for whether they spoke the truth, but the way they spoke to people, whether their public attention to decorum gave evidence of thoughtfulness underneath. When possible, she liked to meet people in person before she made up her mind about them. Grandma wanted to see whether supposed leaders acted the same with ordinary individuals as they did with other powerful leaders or in front of cameras and audiences. She found it telling if a politician's behavior was the same when talking to a laborer or a CEO, to one person or a thousand. She appreciated those who at least appeared to do the right thing even when they thought nobody was looking.

That's one reason Grandma found boasters annoying. She felt that wise people would not need to boast of their achievements, instead trusting that their actions would speak for them over time. It is important to talk about our accomplishments when people need or want more information about us. However, for the most part, if a person has a consistent character, others will understand that it took a successful track record to get where they are.

On the other hand, although Grandma believed that actions and words must be consistent, she didn't necessarily believe actions spoke louder than words. To her, words did mean something. Kindness, thoughtfulness, good manners, consideration, appreciation: she believed all these things must show not only in what we do, but also in what we say. Words can lift up or they can cut. Communication is an important tool, the place where thought and action first meet. My grandma taught me to weigh both words and actions, both in myself and in others.

Actions don't speak louder than words, and words don't speak louder than actions. When the volume is the same, you'll know you're on the path to honesty.

Accepting the Truth

It's not enough for a wise person to be honest if she cannot accept honesty from others. All our grandmas probably said some version of this at one time or another: "Don't dish it out if you can't take it." My grandma put it this way: "A wise person knows how to accept the truth graciously, even when it hurts." That does not mean that every time someone offers to tell you what's wrong with you it's your duty to sit there and take it. Sometimes we have to process criticism for a while, without taking it in and personalizing it, before we decide whether to accept it or not.

When I'm confronted with painful criticism, I find it works best for me if I hear the other person out. Then, without either caving in or lashing out, I simply say, "Let me think about that." Afterward, I do just that. If I conclude that apologies and amends are owed, I take responsibility. If I conclude that the other person is mistaken, I tell him I don't accept his criticism and make my case. If the other person insists on being right, I don't bother with pointless confrontation. I move on.

Whatever honesty people drop on me, whether I like it or not, my goal is to remain open to what is being shared. That's part of maintaining the sort of truth and decorum that my grandma demonstrated in her life. My grandma did not lose her temper because someone told her something she did not want to hear. I suppose she might have gotten upset once or twice in my presence, but her demonstrations of frustration were controlled and directed. Wisdom taught her to let a lot go, even when someone's words made her feel aggravated. "Don't try to make someone feel guilty for sharing the truth with you," she once told me. "If they're willing to tell you what you don't want to hear, they will likely be honest with you in the future."

That doesn't just hold true with criticism, but with all unwanted information. I remember one day I was getting ready to do some baking, and I noticed that all my chocolate chips were gone.

"Does anybody know what happened to the chocolate chips?" I asked my family, suspicious. "How did they disappear?"

Brooke, my ten-year-old, confessed, "Oh, Mommy, I have to tell you. I ate all the chocolate chips."

I remained calm as I nodded. "I kind of thought so."

"But aren't you happy that I could tell you the truth?" she said.

I shot her a wry look and said, "Sure, okay, but you're buying more chocolate chips."

I still made her take responsibility by giving up money from her allowance, but there was also the beauty of realizing that I was raising a daughter who would be honest with me, partly because it was a value Dylan and I had taught her. Because I accepted the fate of the chocolate chips calmly, she understood that she could always tell me the truth and trust that she would not lose my love and acceptance. That's one important reason a person not only needs to tell the truth, but also needs to accept it from others. The trust we're building is mutual.

Don't Mistake Cruelty for Honesty

"Be careful about the words you say to people. Because even if you say you're sorry, you can't take them back." That was a common bit of wisdom from my grandma. She disliked when cruel people used the excuse, "I'm just being honest." Honesty is about giving people the information they need without lying. If you're saying something that may be hurtful or that has an ulterior motive, be careful, because words that cut deep are remembered. Every time you want to share a negative piece of information, especially if it has strong emotion attached, it pays to ask yourself, "Do I really want this person to remember me for saying this? Do I want this to be the moment with me that they never forget?"

That's why my grandmother was cautious with her words and only spoke after at least a moment of deliberation. Whenever she had a disagreement with my grandpa and needed time to reflect or try to understand his position, she would remain silent for a while before she responded. That's when we'd hear the pots getting banged around in the kitchen more than usual as she prepared the next meal. I knew early on that these were simply the sounds of Grandma struggling with Grandpa's point. She was a fast thinker, but a cautious and deliberate talker. She was determined to only speak the truth. More than that, she was determined to only speak the truth *that was helpful.* She was not into full disclosure if she didn't think it would help someone.

I'm sure Grandma would have shaken her head at all the personal travails, opinions, and criticism that many people seem to feel compelled to report on Facebook and Twitter. To her, if it was going to cause someone pain, and if that person was unlikely to feel better or improve because of it, why would you do that? The only rationalization left would be that you wanted to relieve your feelings at someone else's expense.

Grandma and I mostly spoke on the phone, but even though there was typically nobody else around to hear us, she taught me to be careful with my words. This wasn't just a matter of us not hurting other people. Maybe they'd never find out. Rather, it was about not bringing down the level of our humanity, not allowing our characters to sink so low as to find pleasure in the trouble or flaws of others.

If I was having a problem at work, Grandma preferred me not to say, "I spoke to some fool who was rude, insulting, and pigheaded." It wasn't necessary for me to insult that person and try to prove I was right and he was wrong just so she could help me wallow in my misery. She wanted to know what the plain, unvarnished problem was and how she could help me solve it. So instead I would say something like, "I met the most unfortunate person. He used terrible words when we were working together and made it unpleasant. He made it clear that he thought my ideas were lackluster before I even had a chance to explain them. And he put down other people we work with even though they weren't there to defend themselves." I've always done my best to talk this way with everyone, but even when I was tempted to veer from it because someone made me hot under the collar, Grandma's noble behavior always shamed me out of it.

She always reminded me, "You're a bigger person than this. Don't demean yourself by stooping to that level, no matter what someone did to you."

Grandma suggested that anytime you want to make a good impression on people, you do better if you never try to build yourself up by tearing others down. When you resort to insults or accusations, the person who is listening has to wonder why you need to do that: doesn't your argument have enough weight on its own? The next thing they may begin to wonder is whether you're likely to talk about them that way someday when you don't agree with them. She used to say that if you explain your story in straightforward terms, the story is easier to understand and more believable.

Speaking honestly is tricky. That's not because recognizing the truth is hard, but because it can be hard to speak it in such a way that the other person can fully hear and understand your meaning and intent. Grandma believed that if you put thought and care into how you say something, you can deliver a boatload of bad news and the other person will accept it as a caring gift. This requires spending time and energy getting to know other people and how they feel and react to things. It also requires spending time and energy thinking before you speak.

The Difference Between Polite Silence and Withholding

Sometimes the truth just cannot be dressed up. It's going to hurt. Then you have to decide: how important is it? If you're wise, you'll also consider: Is the other person ready for the truth or not?

Some people just can't accept the truth about their flaws or mistakes. With such people, we have to evaluate whether telling them the truth is a productive use of our time and energy. Grandma gave this a lot of thought. She said that the quality of communication was largely driven by how receptive the audience was. What is this person or group going to do with my honesty? Are they going to respond to it by adjusting their behavior, correcting their mistake, or at least acknowledging my position? Or will it just make them angry, damage our relationship, and yield no good results?

Sometimes I'm bursting at the seams with knowledge about how to help someone. I would like to be of service and help them, and when I can I do. But when I can see that nothing good is likely to come of my putting in my two cents, then I just bundle up my honest notion and pack it away. You might believe that wisdom would tell me to let it go. That I don't do. Grandma taught me that wisdom doesn't tell us to erase the information we have that we can't find a use for, but instead to put it away for a rainy day. I might take a lifetime to use it or it may never be used. But, there it will stay, safely tucked away, ready to be of service.

Patience is an important part of honesty: knowing when the timing is right so that your message will be received.

My grandma kept a lot to herself not because she was dishonest, but because she cared about how people felt and she cared about results. Maybe it was Depression Era thinking, too, that she didn't want to ever waste anything, not even words. Whether she was cooking, keeping the books for the family business, or talking to me about life, she always wanted to project the best of herself, and to give others the opportunity to do the same. With Grandma, what you saw and what you heard was what you got. That's as honest as it gets.

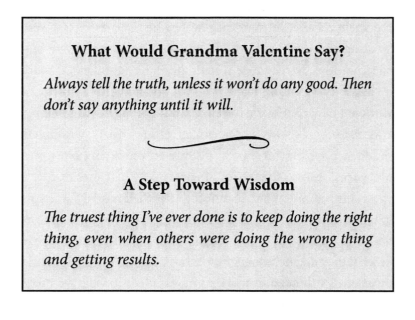

What Would Grandma Valentine Say?

Always tell the truth, unless it won't do any good. Then don't say anything until it will.

A Step Toward Wisdom

The truest thing I've ever done is to keep doing the right thing, even when others were doing the wrong thing and getting results.

Wise People Do the Work

*"A dream doesn't become reality through magic;
it takes sweat, determination and hard work."*
– Colin Powell

As long as there have been humans, we have had work to do. Initially, it was the work of pure survival: foraging and hunting for food and water, avoiding predators, and seeking shelter. Later, human subsistence became more focused: farming and raising livestock, building homes, and creating communities. In recent centuries, humans have created more intricate economies that have complicated the concept of work but have also made life easier: adding the buying, selling, and trading of goods and services to our efforts, which has made it possible for many people to enjoy luxuries and pleasures beyond the basics of survival.

Industrialization and technology have led modern humans to a point where more people than ever have the time, education, and inclination to seek higher-level meaning and purpose in what they do, including and perhaps especially: work. While most of us still need to work to make a living, we have more opportunities than ever to choose how that living is made. Even before now, work has always provided individuals with the opportunity to create a sense of self-worth, build a social network, strengthen community, and participate in society. A wise person would conclude that if one wants to be a fully participating human with a meaningful future, one must embrace work.

So it's dismaying that a number of studies reveal that the Millennial generation, young people born since the 1980s, show a marked disinterest in the value of work and its rewards. Sure, every generation has bemoaned the lack of values of the generations that follow it. But the evidence for the new generation's apathy is not just anecdotal, it's empirical. In 2010, the Pew Research Center released an extensive report on Millennials, also known as Generation Next or Gen Y. In answer to the question, "What makes your generation unique?" at least 10% each of Generation X, Baby Boomers, and the Silent Generation (65 and older) mentioned "work ethic." But "work ethic" did not even make the list for Millennials.

"Our youth now love luxury. They have bad manners, contempt for authority; they show disrespect for their elders and love chatter in place of exercise; they no longer rise when elders enter the room; they contradict their parents, chatter before company; gobble up their food and tyrannize their teachers."
– Socrates

Just because so many Millennials have a disaffected attitude toward work does not meant they are carefree. On the contrary. They suffer from more stress, anxiety disorders, and depression than any other generation, according to a 2012 poll. The poll, conducted by Harris Interactive for the American Psychological Association, surveyed 2,020 U.S. adults 18 and older. On a 10-point scale, all those polled reported their stress at an average of 4.9. But for Millennials, that average was 5.4. What did they name as their primary source of stress? Seventy-six percent cited *work* as the biggest cause of stress in their lives!

Of course, the economy is still relatively bleak after the recent downturn. Unemployment among Millennials is very high at 13%, and even higher if you consider that many Millennials are not counted as unemployed because they've given up looking for jobs. That doesn't explain why those who *do* have jobs are so stressed out.

Why would Millennials have low interest in work, but get stressed out by work? I believe the answer is pretty obvious if you look at the question. They're stressed out by work because they don't recognize work as valuable—and I don't mean in terms of a paycheck. Doing any job is stressful when you have not learned to equate effort with value, action with reward, work with meaning. I believe meaning is what they yearn for. Meaning is what all of us yearn for, once our basic survival needs are met.

Today's employees are seeking a greater sense of meaning from work, the activity where they spend most of their time. According to a 2012 white paper by Nina M. Ramsey, chief human resources officer at Kelly Services: of 170,000 employees surveyed across 30 countries, two-thirds were planning to switch organizations within the year. Ramsey's report goes on to say that fewer than half of employees surveyed said they felt job fulfillment. Most reported that their work does not provide them with a genuine sense of purpose or meaning. Kelly Services' research showed that employees find meaning in work when they feel valued by their employers, are happy in what they do, have opportunities to develop their skills, form bonds with coworkers, and feel connected to an organization's purpose.

One of Kelly Services' aims is to help employers with recruitment, but the way I look at it the company's report aims in two directions: at both employers *and* employees. Employers share some responsibility for engaging their workers in meaningful pursuits. However, employees also have a personal responsibility to find meaning in the work they pursue. I believe this dynamic also holds true in contractor-client relationships.

Those of us who practice wisdom realize that we must perform work if we want to participate in the world. We further realize that we will die a little inside every day unless we find meaning in our participation. Working for money will help us survive, but only working with meaning will help us to truly live.

We Are What We Do

For most of my mom's childhood, my grandpa was beset by stomach issues, probably ulcers, which left him bedridden at one point. So my grandma went back to work and became the family's sole provider for a time. My grandparents never saw it as solely the man's or the woman's job to be the family provider. They saw that as a shared responsibility. They might seem a little ahead of their time to some, but I think they were simply exhibiting an old-fashioned family value that gets expressed differently at different times. Throughout their marriage, whoever was available went out to work, or helped around the house, or both. There was an attitude that you did what you needed to do. In fact, my family was so used to thinking of work as a shared responsibility, that working side-by-side was a measure of family togetherness.

The family that works together, stays together.

The value of working together was so ingrained in our family that, to this day, my family's idea of a vacation is doing work for *ourselves* as opposed to doing work for our employers or clients. A day off just doesn't feel complete to me unless I've done some sort of home improvement project, or made something for the kids, or run an important errand.

I remember when Dylan came with me for his first visit to my mother's tree farm in Michigan, which was originally owned by Grandma and Grandpa. Dylan and I had decided to join my family there for a vacation. When we arrived, Mom said, "Oh, Dylan, I'm so happy to see you! Here's a posthole-digger. I need two posts right over there. They're for the gate we're going to install for the driveway."

In my mind that was no big deal, but Dylan later confessed to me, "I was thinking maybe we'd go golfing or something, you know, do the things that people do on vacation."

"Yeah, that's not the way my family gets together. We work."

Dylan actually had fun. It might sound as if we're people who don't live a balanced life, but I see wisdom in our family's approach to work. To me, what I choose to do when I'm working for a client or an employer allows me to express my values through service to others, but what I choose to work at when I'm relaxing allows me to express myself through what I do for my family and me.

In modern society, we make sharp distinctions between work and leisurely pursuits, but in primitive cultures people did not distinguish between the two. The idea was to work, rest, and play as the need arose, and infuse it all with cultural rites and traditions that made every activity an opportunity for creative expression and community bonding. If you do it all with humility and joy, does it matter what it's called? That's the wisdom my grandma and grandpa passed on to my family, and I'm proud to carry their wisdom forward in what I do.

Wisdom Takes Effort

A lazy person does not feel the need to collect knowledge or, if he does happen to collect knowledge, to act on it. Lazy people try to get away with doing as little as possible for as much reward as possible—and I'm not talking about efficiency. Efficiency would not sacrifice quality just to shorten the process. My point is about the amount of effort one puts into amassing wisdom. If lazy people receive no rewards after doing as little as possible, they tend to blame others. If they receive small rewards, they may manage to survive, but will never learn the gift of true achievement. If they receive greater rewards than they've earned, they often receive little pleasure from it. Even if they manage to have a wealthy time of it despite not earning their way in the world, they may find themselves alone, or with very few friends, because nobody relies on them or trusts them.

Activities that don't exercise the mind and require only a low level of effort, like non-stop video gaming or excessive TV watching, reduce the ability of people to reach their potential or derive pleasure from life. People who have found great joy in developing wisdom are seldom lazy, because they know life is short and that there is much to explore and achieve in that short time.

We can either be passive or active participants in our lives. For the wise person, work is not drudgery but an opportunity to participate. When someone values wisdom, every piece of information, every person, every challenge encountered becomes an opportunity for knowledge, experience, and action. When someone is lazy, anything that challenges that person to think or act seems like an inconvenience.

Although living a meaningful life takes effort, it does not take a genius-level IQ to make a mark in the world and forge a path to a joyful, successful life. Satisfaction in life comes from one thing: a willingness to do the work to pursue the dreams we feel passionate about. Gifted people can be lazy or they can be wise. Wise people, who tend to be successful people, have one thing in common: they do what other people are unwilling to do. Wisdom is not about being the best and brightest, but about persevering. Of course, if you persevere long enough you may become one of the best and brightest. It all starts with a willingness to put whatever brains you have to work.

A well-fed cat may turn lazy. He sees a mouse and bats at it playfully, while a hungry cat chases it down. A wise person is hungry for knowledge, wanting to feed his or her brain the way that hungry cat wants to feed his empty belly. When the great idea appears, the wise person doesn't say, "That's nice, but it's not for me." Instead that person begins to study the idea, chasing down all the possibilities to find out where they lead.

When a wise person pursues a goal, he or she doesn't just engage in the fun parts of the work required. Instead, the wise person understands that even the most exciting and interesting pursuits might require many mundane tasks. The wisdom is in seeing the big picture in those small moments, in recognizing that even the boring steps are part of an exciting whole. Climbing a mountain is not fun in the individual steps, which leave lungs breathless, muscles sore, and the mind exhausted. Still, the climber finds joy in testing the strength and endurance of his or her body, witnessing the awe in nature's rugged beauty, and achieving satisfaction by meeting the challenge of reaching the top. As arduous as a climb may be, the climber recognizes many potential rewards.

A Labor of Love

When wise people work, they don't just see the job itself, but what it says about them, what it says about their caring for others, what it says about their relationship to themselves and the world around them. In that way, all work can be a labor of love. Love is not just a feeling, it is an action. When love is unexpressed through inaction, it diminishes and shrinks like any unused muscle. When love is expressed through action, through hard work, it grows: it grows us, it supports others, it improves the world.

Even the most repetitive work can be joyful, when wisdom teaches us to fill it with meaning. I keep a list of rotating chores for my girls, checking off several items for them to do each week. The chores are not just busywork but important tasks that contribute to the household in a meaningful way, even though some of the duties require no special skills. I keep their chores age-appropriate but not too easy. I want them to understand that they are part of a household, part of a team. This idea of working for the benefit of the group will be important when they start their own households, join their own communities, and take on jobs. I believe that parents do their children a disservice when they make chores too easy or don't give them at all. If you want children to learn the rewards of work, it should be challenging.

BROOKE AND MORGAN: TO-DO LIST

_____ USE BONA CLEANING SYSTEM IN FAMILY
ROOM & HALLWAY

_____ WIPE DOWN WOOD AT RAILING BASE
AND BANNISTER

_____ CLEAN GLASS FRONT DOOR

_____ WIPE DOWN KITCHEN CABINETS AND
BASEBOARDS

_____ SWEEP AND USE BONA ON KITCHEN FLOOR

_____ VACUUM BASEMENT FAMILY ROOM

_____ SWEEP FRONT TILE FLOOR (IN "FOYER"
BY FRONT DOOR) & MOP

_____ DUST LIVING ROOM AND DINING ROOM
(ALSO MAIL TABLE)

_____ SWEEP AND MOP BACK HALL, LAUNDRY AND
MAIN FL BATHROOM

_____ WIPE DOWN BATHROOM COUNTER IN GIRLS'
BATHROOM

_____ WIPE DOWN GUEST BATHROOM COUNTER
(2ND FLOOR)

_____ SWEEP MOMMY AND DADDY'S BATHROOM
FLOOR

_____ WIPE DOWN 1ST FLOOR BATHROOM SURFACES

_____ CLEAN ALL DOOR HANDLES WITH CLOROX WIPES

_____ DUST FAMILY ROOM

_____ SWEEP FRONT PORCH

_____ USE SCRUBBING BUBBLES TO CLEAN TILES AND
TUB IN GIRLS' BATHROOM

_____ USE BONA CLEANING SYSTEM IN LIVING ROOM
AND DINING ROOM

_____ DUST BASEBOARD ON FIRST FLOOR

_____ VACUUM YOUR OWN BEDROOM

_____ VACUUM MOMMY & DADDY'S BEDROOM

_____ VACUUM AREA RUGS IN LIVING RM, DINING RM
& FAMILY RM, OFFICE

I rarely let the girls just sit around the house unless that too has an important goal, such as reading, family bonding, or rest. The value of work is not something kids pick up by osmosis. We definitely have had to demonstrate and explain it to our girls. At first, all the training meant that I was actually doing more work than I had before they started helping me, which is probably why a lot of parents give up and just do it themselves. I understand this urge. But my job at home is not just to keep a household running, it's also to raise future adults with solid values who will become productive members of society. So I had to tough it out through some whining and

262 | Legacy of Wisdom

some poorly executed work. Meanwhile, they had to put up with some criticism and a few of my fits when they tried to get away with "I'll do it later," or "But, Mommy, I *did* clean the floor," even though the floor was still covered with threads, crumbs, dust bunnies, and other particulates.

Passing on the value of work is not a one-way street. As my daughters learn, I learn too. Parents are not born knowing how to parent, after all. It's on-the-job training. One night my younger daughter let me know that I had not yet given her enough information to understand what this chore business was all about. We have family movie night every week, when we all pile into recliner seats in front of the big-screen TV in our basement "theatre." It's a lot of fun.

But this time, after the movie was over, when I was ushering the girls up to bed, Morgan turned to me with a serious look on her face and said, "Mommy, I really need to speak to you."

"What is it?"

"You have to come with me."

"Okay..." I said, curious. I followed her to her room, where she insisted we shut all the doors for privacy, even the closet door. When every last door was shut, I said, "What's going on?"

We sat on her bed, and she looked me in the eye and said, "Mommy, all I do Monday through Friday is wake up, go to school, do homework, and go to sleep. Then on weekends, all I do is wake up, do chores, and go to sleep. What kind of life is this?"

It was tempting to feel guilty, but I was more concerned that she had failed to see the need for her to contribute to the family. Dylan and I had discussed the idea of chores quite thoroughly, so it was important that she understood the why behind it. Still, I realized her interpretation of chores was very real for Morgan.

So I said, "Do you know what your other job is, and what you've failed to do?"

"No..."

"You've failed to find value in everything you do. Don't you understand that everything you're learning now is to prepare you for a very successful and happy life? Even the chores Daddy and I give you?"

You might be surprised to learn that she did not rail at this, but instead reacted with a big smile and simply said, "Oh!"

She just needed me to help her understand that what she was doing now was going to give her rewards later. She just needed me to help her see that work has meaning. Once I gave her a glimpse of what the meaning was supposed to look like, she began to see it for herself.

The next day Morgan and Brooke had chores to do. Whatever they don't get done by the end of Saturday, they have to finish on Sunday. That Sunday, I had to give them back their list because it was very incomplete. This particular Sunday was also their day to go out with Daddy and do something fun. So they had a lot of incentive to get their chores done early, because Daddy always checks in, "Hey, did you get your chores done so we can go out and have fun?"

This time I didn't get one complaint from the peanut gallery, saying, "Oh, my gosh, we have sooooo much work!" In fact, Brooke even said, "I'm working so fast because I need to get all of this done so I can go out with Daddy." What a reversal! They were not bemoaning what they had to do, but realizing that their hard work would lead to a reward. A coveted reward...time with their very fun Daddy.

Dylan is fantastic at parenting as a team, which is part of how we put our work ethic into action at home. He also recognizes the value of teaching the girls a work ethic, even if it means sometimes he misses out on a few playtime moments with them. He would rather miss a few fun times and have hard-working children, than play every day and end up with lazy kids who sit around expecting to be waited on hand and foot.

My grandma often talked about the value of a "good, hard day's work." Work or, more to the point, expending effort, is directly linked to developing one's purpose. Expending effort in all areas of our lives becomes easier when we understand that a work ethic is the first necessary step to finding meaning.

Effort is Good for You

In this age of technology, people have come to value expediency. Quick, easy, and convenient isn't all bad. In fact, it has made our lives better in many ways. But it becomes a problem when we choose expediency at the expense of other things we value. Fast foods, processed foods, and microwaves are more convenient, but we don't want to give up nutrition, or our connection to the earth that provides our sustenance, and the opportunity for family bonding over meal preparation. TV is fun, but we don't want to give up reading and conversation. The Internet offers a wealth of information, communication, and business opportunities, but we don't want to give up diligent research, face-to-face interaction, and the spirit of personal service.

Technology can reduce our workload and give us more time for meaningful new pursuits. But the wise person understands that the shortest distance between A and B isn't always the most satisfying path. Many things in life may grow easier, but wisdom itself is not easy. Wisdom will always require work, because it takes time and effort to accumulate knowledge, develop emotional intelligence, and practice compassion. It takes work to become the best of ourselves, which no high-speed technology can duplicate.

My grandma took advantage of all situations as opportunities to share a philosophy or value with us grandkids, especially activities in the kitchen. Thinking back, the parallels to more complicated situations in life seem countless. One year, after my mom remarried, she and her new husband went on a trip, and Grandma and Grandpa came over to stay with us. Grandma wanted to make chocolate chip cookies. Grandpa was a huge fan of ice cream and cookies, and so were my brothers and me, so it was very easy to get all of us on board.

I enjoyed working with Grandma in the kitchen, mostly helping her find the various appliances and ingredients she would need. By then, the late seventies, many kitchen appliances were electric, and fewer and fewer baking activities required manual effort. However, my grandma did not want to use the electric mixer that day. She taught me a value I carry with me to this day. Some things are best made the old way, with more effort: in this case, hand-mixing. It was her belief that the electric mixer either mixed too little or too much and the cookies did not taste the same.

Hand-mixing cookie dough adds both time and manual effort. You have to cream the butter and brown sugar until silky smooth, then mix in the eggs, vanilla, dry ingredients, and finally the chocolate chips. Using an electric mixer reduces the butter-sugar mixing time alone by a third. So in my adult years, I once tried making Grandma's recipe with the more efficient electric mixer. After that, I went back to hand-mixing, and never made them the faster way again. Grandma had a point; for some reason the hand-mixed version really was better.

To this day, I make chocolate chip cookies by hand, although I do make other types of cookies with the electric mixer. It has become something of a tribute to my grandma's teachings about the value of effort. I've taught my daughters the hand-mixing way and told them the reason why. We'll see if they're ever swayed to grab the electric mixer. For now, they do it the hand-mixing way too, and they love it, sharing special time and effort in the kitchen and enjoying the reward of eating their favorite cookies.

How We Value Work

Many of today's corporate leaders put expediency before such values as creativity, quality, or loyalty. I have been saddened over the past three decades to see how many businesses have decided that laying people off is an expedient way to improve their bottom line, as opposed to developing new revenue streams when possible. This is not only bad for the laid-off employees and their families, but also bad for companies.

Ever since downsizing became a buzzword in the eighties, many employees have developed a distrust of company owners and managers, and many consumers have demonized many large companies. In this way, a corporate emphasis on quick-fix expediency above creative new ideas has caused a rift in employer/employee loyalty as well as company/ customer loyalty. Laying off workers and expecting those who remain to pick up the slack may be a fast way to make money, but it does not contribute to long-term economic growth and opportunity, whether for businesses or their workers. The key to long-term profitability is to make the pie bigger, not smaller.

What makes the pie bigger is not laying employees off, but instead inviting them to be creative. Creativity is the path to identifying new revenue streams through new products, services, and production efficiencies. The challenge is for company leaders to ideate on the universe of options instead of grabbing at low-hanging fruit. Creating options takes time, effort, and a willingness to invest resources. It also requires a healthy amount of wisdom to predict viability and outcomes. Applying wisdom to a problem can create new ideas and prevent layoffs. So why have layoffs become the norm? Because wisdom takes time, effort, and a willingness to accept risk. In short, it's not easy.

My grandmother saw the writing on the wall before she died. I'm sure she would not have been surprised by the Great Recession. She often told me that our economy was in trouble if decision makers didn't start thinking in human terms: about making things and pursuing ideas to fulfill human needs, about creating opportunities for humans to work and lead. Because she so deeply believed in human ingenuity, she also believed in capitalism, in mankind's ability to create and succeed. Entrepreneurship and capitalism are what made this country great, but we've allowed a few bad apples to spoil the whole bunch, tarnishing the meaning and inspiration that arise from these two philosophies.

I remember saying, "Grandma, I can understand if an industry is contracting and all of a sudden it's, 'Do we let the company go under or do we let off a few people?' But you have to communicate that you've exhausted every other possibility. Then you have to explain to your employees, many of whom have families, that you've done everything possible."

My grandma put it more simply: "There's a better way to handle it. Most definitely. Once you create that ill will, once you destroy that trust, it's hard to undo the damage." Creating distrust interferes with people finding their value through work, especially if corporate leaders send out clear messages that employees and their work are not valuable.

Do you know what happens when companies give careful thought to treating employees as team members? Businesses that engage their employees to contribute, encouraging two-way communication and sharing of ideas, succeed at a much higher rate than their competition. According to an article in the December 2010 issue of the *International Journal of Business and Management*, written by PhD scholar Solomon Markos and Professor M. Sandhya Sridevi of Andhra University's Department of Commerce and Management Studies: "…the more engaged employees are, the more likely their employer is to exceed the industry average in its revenue growth. Employee engagement is found to be higher in double-digit growth companies."

People who value work do not expect companies to make them rich. They just want an opportunity to offer something of value. When people feel valued, it makes them excited to get up in the morning and go to work.

Still, that value has to start within. Each of us must value himself enough to believe he has something to contribute, and value others enough to contribute it. Wisdom is not just something that sits silently within. Wisdom does not fulfill its purpose until it takes action, and action is what makes the world go around.

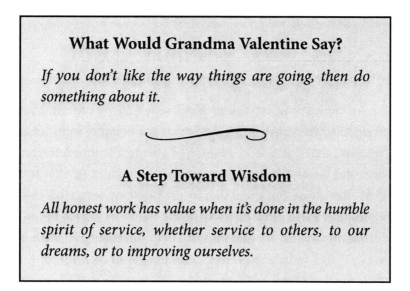

What Would Grandma Valentine Say?

If you don't like the way things are going, then do something about it.

A Step Toward Wisdom

All honest work has value when it's done in the humble spirit of service, whether service to others, to our dreams, or to improving ourselves.

Think for Yourself

*"To thine own self be true, and it must follow, as the night
the day, thou canst not then be false to any man."*
– William Shakespeare

Independent Thought versus Groupthink

For decades now, studies have repeatedly revealed that
group brainstorming is not the best way to inspire individual
creativity, that if you send a bunch of people off alone to create
ideas and solutions, they'll come up with much more effective
ideas than if you put them in a room together. Yet to this day,
businesses and committees still react with excitement and
optimism when someone shouts, "Let's brainstorm!" Such is
our yearning to belong. While belonging is a beautiful aspect
of community, and brainstorming can be effective for some
purposes, it is my experience that discussions with others are
best only after individual thinking and reflection are done.

A study recently published in *Applied Cognitive Psychology*,
by Nicholas W. Kohn of the University of Texas at Arlington
and Steven M. Smith of Texas A&M, has piled on yet more
evidence that group brainstorming is not the best strategy to
generate unique and varied ideas. The researchers concluded

that group brainstorming exercises often lead to fixation on one idea or possibility, blocking out other ideas and possibilities. The result is a conformity of ideas. According to Kohn, "Fixation to other people's ideas can occur unconsciously and lead to you suggesting ideas that mimic your brainstorming partners. Thus, you potentially become less creative."

For the study, groups of four people used AOL Instant Messenger as an electronic discussion format to share ideas, while other groups of two to four people brainstormed ideas individually. In both cases, the groups sat in the same room, separated by dividers, but did not speak to each other. The group that shared ideas did so anonymously via the AOL chat function. In one experiment, the groups who worked individually without sharing ideas generated 44% more ideas in the first five minutes. Over time, that effect diminished, but even by the end of the session they still generated 16% more ideas than their counterparts who shared information. The effects were similar for their other experiments.

When William H. Whyte coined the term Groupthink in 1952, he was not just referring to instinctive conformity but to "a rationalized conformity—an open, articulate philosophy which holds that group values are not only expedient but right and good as well." Today people often use Groupthink to refer to any kind of thinking that reflects the group rather than the individual. In either case, it's real. Even if we want to benefit the group, we best do so when we think for ourselves first. It is important to bring our individual ideas to a group.

Of course, if we can't win over a group with our individual ideas, those ideas won't go far. However, if groups are aware of the group fixation phenomenon, Kohn and Smith suggest that knowledge may help them find ways to prevent conformity, such as giving individuals an opportunity to break away to do individual work and then return to groups with a fresh perspective.

When I worked for a management consulting firm in Chicago, we sought solutions to needs identified by various consumers or industrial groups. Whether we were trying to help consumers more effectively moisturize skin or help an electric utility develop solutions to electrical surges and sags at their industrial customers' facilities, we were very intentional in our approach to putting together many different focus groups, typically groups of eight to ten people. Simply putting people together and asking for an answer can result in consensus-building and restricted ideation. However we designed a variety of safeguards into the process to help us avoid Groupthink, such as: seeking participants with a broad variety of backgrounds, thoughtfully addressing the group with the expectation that individual differences existed and that we needed to hear all viewpoints, and specifically and clearly instructing each group not to adapt or jump on the bandwagon of the most popular solution.

To me, studies into the risks of Groupthink and the limitations of group brainstorming simply confirm what experience, intuition, and Grandma have all taught me: the importance of thinking for ourselves. Not only does it serve our individual development, but the creativity it engenders is a benefit to society. Odd, isn't it? That individuality ultimately gives us the great ideas that move humans forward as a group.

"A 'collective' mind does not exist. It is merely the sum of endless numbers of individual minds. If we have an endless number of individual minds who are weak, meek, submissive and impotent—who renounce their creative supremacy for the sake of the 'whole' and accept humbly that 'whole's' verdict—we don't get a collective super-brain. We get only a weak, meek, submissive and impotent collective mind."
– Ayn Rand

Don't Take Someone Else's Word for It

Relying on others is sometimes a requirement to get things done, but as Ronald Reagan was famous for saying, "Trust, but verify." One reason it's so important to verify, is that many people present their assumptions as fact.

It's good that there are a few things that we can typically rely on, because most people don't have the luxury of time and energy to double-check the reliability of everything we think we know. For example, if you're a taxpaying American, when you send your U.S. federal income tax payment to the IRS do you send it via certified mail? Probably not. Most people don't. Americans are used to dropping their envelopes and packages in the U.S. mail and we walk away confident that they will get to their destination. Chances are they probably will. This was Benjamin Franklin's vision when he structured the U.S. Postal Service in the late 1700s. It has been one of the most reliable organizations established by the founders of the

United States, despite its management and financial woes over the past few decades. In general, though, there are few things that we can rely on with that much trust. So we have to sort through what we have time to check and what we have to take on faith.

I was project manager for the 2002 Chicago Innovation Awards, and I personally went through each nomination to verify the information submitted. There were dozens of applications that covered a variety of new products and services. A fellow consultant and I were ultimately responsible for confirming the information supplied. We checked sources and conducted interviews to ensure the accuracy of all the applications, We did not have the luxury of relying on the applicant data, not because the submitters were dishonest, but because we were giving out awards and recognition based on tangible criteria. It had to be verified or the integrity of the awards would be risked.

In a busy world, there must be times when we choose to "take someone's word for it." Making assumptions is something humans do to get through everyday life without making themselves crazy. But sometimes the stakes are too high. Knowing when to accept an assumption, and when not to, requires the wisdom to weigh the risks. Young children can be led to believe the most fantastic stories because assumptions and facts are one and the same in their world. They have not yet seen enough examples of assumptions turning out to be untrue.

Early in my childhood, I did not fully understand my parents' divorce. After they split, I did not see my father very often, and thought that limitation was his choice. After my stepfather adopted us, we no longer saw my father and I thought that was his choice too. It was in my teenage years that I felt a need to reach out to my father and ask him what really happened. I wanted to understand him more directly.

What I learned was completely different than the story I had lived with most of my childhood. My mother never spoke poorly of my father, so I was fully responsible for the assumptions I had made based on what I thought I knew. In the end, I found out that my father had yearned for a relationship with all three of his children and that allowing the adoption was a decision he deeply regretted. Ever since then, I've always taken pause when hearing one side of a situation that involves families, whatever it is. There are always so many unknown events and issues that can change how a situation appears.

> "Everything we hear is an opinion, not a fact.
> Everything we see is a perspective, not the truth."
> — Marcus Aurelius

If we're not careful, it can become all too easy to rely on what others tell us as fact, or to expect others to simply accept whatever we tell them as fact. For example, if I'm talking about a political policy, I might say X, Y, and Z were involved in establishing this policy and that's why it's bad. However, the person I'm speaking to might not think that X, Y, and Z are bad. That's called a false premise. People use them all of the time, especially when they relinquish individual thought and embrace Groupthink. If you're wise, you won't expect the other party to assume that X, Y, and Z were bad just because you say so. Maybe you've done some studying on the matter, or maybe you just trust the information because you received it from someone else who you believe has studied the matter. But that's no reason to assume that the people you're talking to are wrong because they won't accept your word for it. That wouldn't be any wiser of them than it would be of you to assume they were right about something just because they seemed certain.

Throughout life, we receive a lot of conflicting information. Critical thinking is necessary to guide ourselves in reading people, understanding the information we receive, analyzing contradictions, recognizing assumptions, and tying all of the pieces together to create a consistent whole that conveys truth. Only then can we make informed decisions. This is what wisdom is all about.

Independence Isn't Easy

Encouraging a society to develop the leadership, inventions, and creativity that help humanity advance requires independence, or more specifically, independent thought. A society advances when people are free to reach their individual potential. Everyone benefits in some way. I believe that politicians who want government to control all aspects of the lives of American citizens have negatively impacted the independent spirit that built the foundation for our vibrant society of great thinkers. Giving citizens independence paves the way for independent thought. The more that a central government dictates how people are educated, how they earn their way in the world, and how their money and property are spent and used, the less decision-making ability and freedom citizens have.

Grandma was all for helping people get on their feet, and taking care of the elderly and children, but we sometimes discussed what a short hop-skip-and-a-jump it was from compassionate democracy to a very different political structure that diminished the human spirit. In a democratic system, wise people agree to help others by choice. We've seen what happens when choice is taken out of the equation: autocracy, fascism, communism, dictatorship. Grandma and I sometimes talked about the inevitable crushing of independence that will come from an unbridled continuation of the welfare state.

"President Clinton is in the news with his welfare reforms," Grandma said during one such conversation. "It seems that one of the hard points between the politicians is the welfare-to-work requirement."

"Yes," I said. "I've been following, and I watched some interesting analysis on *This Week with David Brinkley.*"

"You know, Gabrielle, politicians made a lot of mistakes during Franklin Roosevelt's New Deal. They continue to assume that people can't be asked to do for themselves. Thankfully we were able to help Aunt Bernice during those tough times so I know support is needed at times, but I do hope they pass welfare-to-work as a requirement. It would be good to make sure people have a sense of urgency to get back on track as soon as they can."

"I agree. It all boils down to showing people you believe they can get back on their feet. Why give endless support—it tells people you have no faith in them. How depressing."

During many a conversation like this, Grandma concluded, "I wonder where it will end?"

Later that year, TANF was passed with the back to work requirement in place. It made Grandma hopeful. She had more respect for people who talked about their troubles as if it were their responsibility to make a plan for improving things, whether their problems were their fault or not. She had a very optimistic view about people and what they could do. Grandma believed that when people were down on their luck they did not need someone to hand them money. What they needed was for someone to believe in them. And what they needed most was to believe in themselves. All of this required independent thought: *What's my problem? What resources do I have to solve it? What's my plan?* If they could get that far, the next step was to begin, without anybody else telling them what to do or how to do it.

"People can do it. Look at me. I only had an eighth-grade education, and I managed. It's not about education or money. It's about using your mind."
– Grandma Valentine

On the other hand, as long as America has a government of, by, and for the people, we will always be riding that fine line between not doing enough and doing too much. So, although it's important to think and do for ourselves and to encourage others to do the same, figuring out what is required from government will always be a challenge. It's a challenge that requires leaders who can combine compassion for people with the ability to engage in critical thinking,

Although my grandmother was concerned that government might try to do too much for people instead of letting them do for themselves, her greater worry was that voters would accept these policies without question just because some politician convinced them it was "good to help people." She was appalled at how often people seemed to assume that something was a good idea, just because someone who was a charismatic speaker packaged it in feel-good words and declared it was so.

Grandma knew that the world wasn't always going to go the way she thought it should, and when it didn't she was willing to hope that she would be proven wrong—that everything would turn out okay despite her misgivings. She did not have a problem with people who disagreed with her either, so long as their opinions were their own. What frustrated her was when she heard people repeat the latest catch phrases and ideas instead of coming up with their own thoughts.

> *"I wish people would think for themselves."*
> – Grandma Valentine

You Know The Right Thing

Even when you think carefully about your options and do your best to do the right thing, there are no guarantees. Wise people often differ in their ideas about which path will truly be of service, whether to other people, to themselves, or to God. We might all agree that we shouldn't just hand a hungry man a fish, but instead teach him to fish. However, while he's learning to fish, should we give him a meal so he can have the strength to reel in his catch, or will hunger be enough to stoke his desire to successfully reel it in? How long do we give him to learn? If he learns but still can't catch anything, what do we do then? Is it our responsibility whether he sinks or swims? If it's not our responsibility, are we better off letting him sink, or might he take us down with him? This can get complicated.

When decisions get complicated, the best we can do is take in all the information, come to our own conclusions, and apply our values to promoting this or that plan of action. Rest assured, other people who are doing the same will still come up with different answers. In the end, sometimes the only wrong choices are to choose against your own values, or to fail to choose at all. Right action does not come with guarantees. This is about doing your best with integrity. It's surprising to me how many people don't get this, how many people let others make decisions for them, refuse to take responsibility for decisions, or blame others for decisions—all because they are too lazy to do the work it takes to create and follow their own moral compass.

Shortly after I completely my MBA, classes in ethics became a popular offering in many programs. A few MBA programs now require them. Although I believe a strong ethical back-bone is important in any profession, except perhaps for a thief, it is curious to me that many young adults take these classes hoping someone will teach them how to do the right thing. If someone reaches adulthood without an understanding about how to demonstrate solid ethics, which includes a basic love and appreciation for others, then something else has failed.

The Center for Youth Ethics at the nonprofit Josephson Institute has come up with its own Six Pillars of Character®, ethical values the center suggests all young people should learn and apply independently to their own situations. This organization came up with these six pillars in the belief that we can all agree on their importance to moral development, regardless of our political affiliation, religious beliefs, cultural backgrounds, or socio-economic status. I love their list:

Six Pillars of Character®

1. Trustworthiness
2. Respect
3. Responsibility
4. Fairness
5. Caring
6. Citizenship

If we put any decision process to the test in terms of how well it adheres to the above six principles, it might not make the final decision any easier, but it certainly makes the process clearer. As I mentioned in Chapter Three, I landed my first job when I was eleven. I was a tennis court monitor for the local park district. When the woman who managed the facilities interviewed me for the position, she had several questions for me. Interestingly, they echoed the Six Pillars above. I remember them because I was a little scared of her. I'm sure she was a kind woman, but she was stern and demanding so a little fear was natural for a young person.

Her first question was definitely about trustworthiness: "I will expect that you can bring the money pouch to my office every day after the courts close if you are the last monitor on the schedule. Can you be trusted to do this?" After that, I can't remember the order of the questions, but they reflected the Six Pillars all the way:

Responsibility: "I expect that you will be on time because I will be waiting for you. Can you make it on time? You will be expected to keep track of the number of people entering with a pass versus cash. And I need you to report these numbers accurately. Can you do this?"

Fairness: "You are not allowed to let your friends or family in for free. Everyone pays for court time. Do you understand?"

Respect: "If I find out that this rule is broken, you can be fired."

Caring: "I expect you to take care of the courts, be courteous, and help out visitors if they have questions."

Citizenship: "Remember, our courts are public. We serve the public. Taxpayers pay for this park facility so we need to respect them and take care of the facility. Do you understand?"

My answer to all of the questions was, "Yes," and I said it in a serious tone that showed I was listening carefully and knew what I was agreeing to do. My decision to take the job was based on my belief that I could live up to everything she asked me to do. It was a simple job, but I took it seriously, always showed up on time, and kept the courts spic-and-span.

Remember, ten people might apply the above six character traits to their decision processes and come up with ten different decisions. That does not prove that these traits are flawed, but rather that they do very well at preserving individual integrity. If a group must come up with a single decision, then the same traits come into play in deciding whose idea to go with.

As we discuss our differences, we still ask: Is our discussion honest? Are we showing each other respect? Are we taking responsibility for our part? Are we all putting our care for each other and others ahead of our egos and personal differences? Are we committed to fully participating as citizens? At the end of such a discussion, it's unlikely anyone will completely get their way, yet if we all remain committed to these six pillars it's likely that there will be some sort of forward movement that will be of more service to people than if we had all just given up and walked away.

I love that the above pillars are all reflected in some form in Grandma's and Benjamin Franklin's values frameworks. I believe that demonstrates how fundamental values are to making decisions for oneself and staying true to one's individual beliefs and thinking.

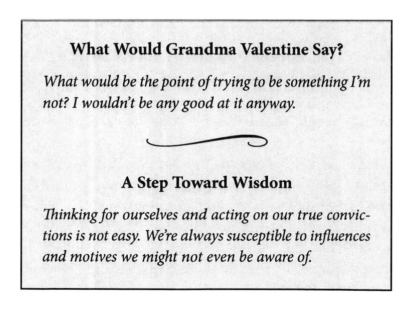

What Would Grandma Valentine Say?

What would be the point of trying to be something I'm not? I wouldn't be any good at it anyway.

A Step Toward Wisdom

Thinking for ourselves and acting on our true convictions is not easy. We're always susceptible to influences and motives we might not even be aware of.

What Our Elders Pass On To Us

"If you associate enough with older people who do enjoy their lives, who are not stored away in any golden ghettos, you will gain a sense of continuity and of the possibility for a full life."
– Margaret Mead

Our Elders Really Are Wiser

Once upon a time, research studies seemed to indicate that mental function declines over time. Later, psychologists from the University of Texas and Texas A&M concluded that the test designs were biased against older brains. So they came up with new tests that revealed the greater wisdom of the older brain. Their findings were published in the journal *Psychological Science* in 2011. While previous studies had focused on people's capacity to make one-time choices, the newer study focused on requiring participants to weigh their choices based on how it would affect future choices, which is the way we make decisions in the real world. The trials revealed that older people's wisdom helps them outperform younger people at making choices that lead to improved long-term gain.

They conducted two experiments. In the first one, the team asked 28 university-age adults and 28 senior adults to perform a decision-making task that required them to think about immediate rewards. As expected, the younger subjects were quicker to make choices that led to instant gratification.

The second experiment revealed a significant switch. This time, about 50 people aged 67 to 82 and about 50 people aged 20 to 36 were asked to figure out how to store oxygen for a virtual mission to Mars. They could choose between an option which would increase rewards in future trials, and one that decreased future rewards but offered a larger immediate one. Older participants far outperformed the rival group by figuring out which option led to the most long-term rewards. The older group was more adept at making strategic decisions that took future possibilities into account. The younger group was less able to see the benefits of planning.

The findings contradict the stereotype of elderly people losing their mental edge. Researchers concluded that, regardless of how long senior citizens take to make a decision, it is typically a better decision than one made in youthful haste. So it seems that senior citizens are the tortoise, and young people the hare.

I always believed this, even when I was a hare. It's why I leaned on my grandma's tortoise advice even when I wanted to jump the gun and race to my reward. The wisdom to stop and think through the long-term ramifications of my present actions instead of going for immediate gratification is a skill my grandmother taught me and my mother echoed. I still pause and listen to people with more experience than me because I know I might learn something.

Now that I have children of my own, I'm becoming a tortoise. Now I believe it's my responsibility to pass the baton on to my young hare apprentices.

Elders Naturally Have More Perspective

Back in my consulting days, when we assembled focus groups to gather insights and information about consumers and their perspectives, I voiced my desire to be the group consultant for the older demographic respondents. I found the 60-plus group to be the most fun. If I was going to ask people personal questions about their likes and dislikes and then ask them to expand on their thoughts, I wanted to work with the crowd that could laugh at the reality of life, at how the little things were fixable and the big things required patience and thought. In the end, there wasn't a 60-plus group I didn't enjoy.

Please don't misunderstand me. I could relate and speak with those who were my age and younger, but with the older people there was a greater richness in the conversations and a livelier humor that popped through on questions that in the scheme of things did not reflect life's greatest challenges. In addition, I felt I gleaned the most information from the older groups. They seemed to have more clarity of thought on many issues, because they had more years of life experience and had spent more time thinking about them. They were also able to distill their concerns and desires in more concrete terms. If a respondent shared that dry skin was painful and that this was reason enough to solve the problem, it usually only took one or two questions for me to get the picture. Younger respondents might have the same opinion, but it would take much longer to pull it out of them.

I most admired the wisdom of the older groups in their sense of perspective. Even though I had to ask them questions about relatively minor issues like dry skin or weight loss, I felt that their priorities were grounded in strong values. I knew that if I wanted to ask them about weight loss, they would want to focus more on health and less on looks. I knew that if I asked about anything related to their fears, they would usually tie back to family, home, and security, not fears involving what other people might think about them. It was typical for a brief sidebar on grandchildren to slip into the otherwise structured conversation, and it warmed me to know how important family relationships were to people who had lived long enough to reflect deeply on what mattered most in life.

Bottom line, our elders tend to naturally fold life's learnings into well-articulated perspectives. So why don't we all use this accumulation of experience to unfold life's mysteries, not about skin care, but about reaching our potentials, dealing with failure, and building resilience? It seems like a logical idea, but one that has been lost in modern America's youth-focused society.

We all have the potential to receive the legacy of those who came before us and extract the pearls of wisdom it contains. The elders we look to for this legacy don't have to be our grandparents. We can look to an elderly neighbor who needs a little assistance getting packages into a car, a senior citizen sitting on a park bench, or an older friend who would love the company. Our elders have something to say about life's questions, big or small, and all that is required of us is a keen ear to pick up the flashes of experience and observation that they have accumulated over the years.

The Gift of Grandparents

My grandmother has had such a lasting influence on the way I make decisions that I imagine I owe a great deal of my joy and success in life to her wisdom. That's why I've made it a priority to foster a relationship between my daughters and their grandparents. They're very fortunate that all four of their grandparents are living, and that each grandparent is a unique individual with special qualities worth learning from.

Although I was closest to my Grandma Valentine, all of my grandparents were important to me. My paternal grandfather passed when I was very young, but my other grandparents shared many special insights and values with me. Some they learned from experiences they had in their own lifetimes, others were passed down to them from previous generations.

When my older daughter, Brooke, was nine we gave her a phone as a gift. Nothing fancy, not a Smartphone, just a phone. People looked at us as if we had lost our minds. If we had bought the phone so that she could text, talk to her friends, and play games at all hours, it certainly would have been out of character, because we're fairly strict about making sure our daughters focus on school, family, chores, active play, and reading—and that they're not glued to technology.

But this phone had a special purpose—though no doubt that will change over time.

Our older daughter was soft-spoken. She was a quiet observer who wasn't given much to either talking or writing. We wanted to encourage her to write and talk more, to learn to express those great thoughts rattling around her mind and heart. We gave her a phone so that she could text and talk to her grandmas and grandpas as a way to practice her communication skills while also developing these key relationships in her life. Some people might say, "But texting is not writing," and I did hesitate on that count. But in the end, it gave her a fun new way to play with words and to connect with others.

What was most important to us was that we were passing on a priority. When we gave her that first opportunity to step into a wider world of communication, she made her first step toward fully developing her grandparent relationships. They are, after all, family members full of experience and wisdom. It was a fun first step, because a grandparent offers a special relationship that is very different from a parent. So she could have this special time that she enjoyed while developing a relationship that would be important to her development as a person.

When we gave her the phone, we programmed just seven numbers into it: all four grandparents, her Daddy, me, and just one friend. It was not a big free-for-all where she could call anyone and everyone and chatter all night. The purpose was focused on developing communication skills and these critical grandparent relationships.

We could have just let her use the regular home phone, but I wanted her to develop a stronger bond with her grandparents, and to me our phone didn't signal that special one-on-one time. When I'm on the phone with my mom and I say, "Okay, here's Brooke," then *I'm* ready to give the phone to Brooke, but is Brooke ready to talk to my mother? I would rather have my daughter develop that thoughtfulness and interest in others that requires her to make the choice, "I think I'm gonna call Grandma Joyce," and then pick up the phone and call her. Having her own phone allows her to listen to her inner priorities and values, and then rely on her own desire to make that connection. It requires her to take the initiative to reach out with a specific purpose and in a specific state of mind. When she calls, it is because she intends to have those conversations.

Our younger daughter, Morgan, also got a phone about a year later, and we encouraged her to use it to stay in touch with her grandparents as well. Our younger daughter was already outgoing, and had always enjoyed checking in with all of the family just to say hello. She loves talking and connecting to people around her and falls into it quite easily. Since the dynamic is different, what drives her phone calling decisions is different. But she too is building important relationships with her elders. And even though Morgan did not need the encouragement to engage, she appreciated having a tool with which to do it on her own terms, when she was feeling the need to connect, especially with her grandparents who mean so much to her.

It's not unusual for Morgan to call her grandpa at the drop of a hat and say, "Hi, Grandpa! What are you doing?" Often he simply tells her what he's doing and she tells him what she's doing, and as fast as she got on the phone she's already signing off, "Well, bye Grandpa!" I'm sure that gives him a chuckle. But for a nine-year-old, that's plenty. It's actually quite a lot. She's reaching out to make a connection and to let someone know she cares. For now, she has simply opened a door. Opened a door to love, and to wisdom. Who knows where that door might lead?

> *"My grandson Sam Saunders has been playing golf since he could hold a club and I spent a lot of time with him over the years. Like my father taught me, I showed him the fundamentals of the game and helped him make adjustments as he and his game matured over the years."*
> — Arnold Palmer

The Next Generation

Wisdom asks us to extend what we know right now, or at least what we perceive, into the future. This was probably easier for my grandma with her ninety-plus years of experience than it is for me even now. By the same token, it's easier for me than it is for my children. This is a never-ending chain, and wise people understand that it is our privilege and our responsibility not to break that chain. Passing on wisdom is tricky, because part of wisdom is sharing what we know so that others can benefit from it, but another part is allowing people to make their own discoveries and their own mistakes so that they can develop as individuals.

I believe it is my responsibility to share my wisdom with the next generation. My daughters are going to figure out many of life's lessons on their own. Many of those lessons I can't get involved with, don't need to get involved with, and truly don't want to get involved with, because I want them to develop the ability to make decisions based on who they are. They have their own beautiful personalities, and in many respects they're better than me. I don't want to impose myself on them and interfere with their unique potential. Understanding the essence of wisdom gives me this understanding.

"Parents can only give good advice or put them on the right paths, but the final forming of a person's character lies in their own hands."
– Anne Frank

Still, there are a few things that I can tell them so they can make better decisions. While they are young, it's still my responsibility to keep them safe and healthy, whether it's ensuring they eat healthy food, helping them get a good education, protecting them, or simply offering them comfort or advice. It is also important for me to encourage those conversations with their elders, so they can investigate life and its possibilities through the eyes of greater experience and wisdom than I can offer.

Wisdom is an empowering gift to pass on, because it allows any individual, any one of us, to figure out life's intricacies and solve problems on our own. In the end, our greatest strength comes from our ability to do for ourselves and develop the self-efficacy and pride that comes from that. Wisdom allows us to solve and to achieve, and to enjoy the feeling of "I did that!"

Love is a Wisdom All Its Own

I am thankful for the lessons I learned from my grandma. She taught me that we are all in a position to pass on wisdom, no matter what our circumstances. Grandma had the quiet confidence that comes from self-sufficiency and a well-developed understanding of life and people. She was confident in her ability to know who she was, to be a good person, and to do the right thing. My grandma was a woman of substance, and that substance was simple. It was a substance that said, "Life is full of challenges, but it's also full of opportunities, curiosities, and those people whom I love. I know who I am and what I'm made of, and with that I have all I need to make a good life."

It's not possible to practice wisdom without having the generosity to love others and the openness to receive love in return. Motivated only by self-interest, our lives would shrink and all its opportunities become meaningless. I suppose it might be possible to love without wisdom, but love without wisdom would likely lead someone to behave in irrational extremes: wasting energy on the unworthy, giving where it is not wanted, or expecting love to solve all one's problems.

My grandmother did none of those things. She understood that love was a gift, not a guarantee. If you wanted to enjoy love, you had to give it away without expectation. She did just that, loving people in a way that never made them feel burdened, only appreciated. Grandma understood that life is lived mostly in the details, in the day-to-day, so that's where she showed her love. Her demonstrations of love were not showy or dramatic. Grandma was one for little gifts, little gestures, and kind words.

Grandma made sure the people she cared about knew that she always had them in her heart and mind. She regularly called her sisters and cousins simply to see how they were.

"Just to say hello," she told them. As she became less mobile, she did not let that stop her from getting around. If visitors came over, she made tea, put out the butter cookies, and insisted they visit for a while. She held onto the manners of yesteryear, traditions I still honor when I can. When I came over, she always raced around to make sure I was fed and comfortable. "Grandma, you don't have to do anything, really. I just stopped over to say hello." But she would ignore my words and keep right on taking care of me.

She sewed me a set of soft handmade pajamas every Christmas until her eyesight began to fail. I loved wearing those jammies, feeling the soft material, reading the little label that said, "Made by Grandma Valentine." I still wear the last thing she ever made me, the Christmas before she died. That year she was really quite blind, so I didn't expect anything. However, several months after Christmas, right after Grandma passed away, my mom gave me a package and excitedly asked me to open it. Inside was a beautiful plush robe. "She worked on it for a long time," Mom told me, "And she had it set aside for a while. I had to finish it for her." Grandma had passed on her sewing skills to my mom, who was also a magnificent seamstress. She showed me the row where Grandma's stitching left off and hers began, reminding me of all we pass on from generation to generation.

"Nothing says love like homemade. And I like making pajamas. The love comes from the things made by my own hands."
— Grandma Valentine

That soft, thick robe still reminds me of my grandmother, and the quiet, unassuming, but sure way that she shared herself, her love, and her wisdom with me.

Such is the wisdom of a grandmother, and it is worth passing on.

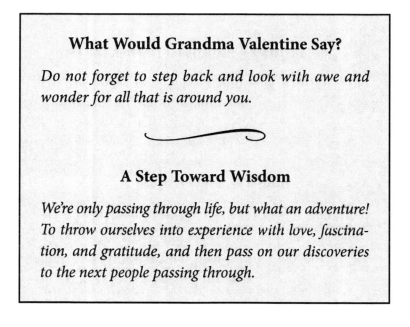

What Would Grandma Valentine Say?

Do not forget to step back and look with awe and wonder for all that is around you.

A Step Toward Wisdom

We're only passing through life, but what an adventure! To throw ourselves into experience with love, fascination, and gratitude, and then pass on our discoveries to the next people passing through.

Conclusion

Pulling It Together, Short and Sweet

What does this all mean? Why do I discuss so many seemingly disparate elements, or what I call dimensions, in the same conversation about wisdom? Because wisdom is complex. Wisdom develops to varying degrees in all of us. However, it is not as simple as the definition from Merriam-Webster would have us believe. It takes developing different aspects of the human condition, mind, and perspective to understand and apply it.

My grandma believed that everyone has the capacity to develop wisdom. It was amazing to her that more people did not find the joy in it. It made her life full when other comforts were lacking. It made life exciting when there was no other form of entertainment. It allowed her to experience the warmth and love resulting from compassion for others. Wisdom was a fundamental thought process to pass on to her heirs as her legacy. It was the most valuable thing she possessed and the source from which she derived the most happiness.

So as you reflect on the different dimensions of wisdom discussed in this book, please know that they do, in fact, belong together. Can they exist separately? Perhaps. But the absence of any of these dimensions will limit one's journey towards one's own wisdom potential.

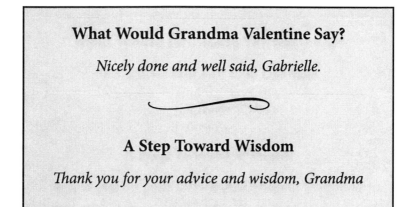

What Would Grandma Valentine Say?

Nicely done and well said, Gabrielle.

A Step Toward Wisdom

Thank you for your advice and wisdom, Grandma

About the Author

Gabrielle V. Taylor leads a strategic management consultancy based in Littleton, Colorado.

Ms. Taylor was previously a management consultant with Kuczmarski & Associates (K&A) in Chicago, Illinois before relocating to Colorado. She specialized in developing new products, services and marketing strategies.

Ms. Taylor's last client engagement at K&A involved launching and managing the 2002 Chicago Innovation Awards sponsored by The Chicago Sun Times and K&A and subsequently sold to the Wrigley Company of Chicago.

Before joining K&A, Ms. Taylor worked for the Morton Salt Company for over nine years. For her outstanding work at Morton, Ms. Taylor was awarded the YWCA Outstanding Business Achievement Award and was inducted into the Salt Crystal Society.

In Colorado, Ms. Taylor recently completed a six-year term on Aspen Academy's Board of Trustees, and served the last three years as Board Chair. Aspen Academy is located in Greenwood Village, Colorado. In 2009, Ms. Taylor graduated from the Leadership Jefferson County program sponsored by the West Chamber in Colorado.

In Illinois, Ms. Taylor was active in the Chicago Chamber of Commerce's Youth Motivation Program as a guest speaker in Chicago public schools. She also has lectured at Notre Dame University on business expansion in Mexico. Other community support included participating in various fundraising activities for the United Way and volunteering at the Anti-Cruelty Society of Chicago.

Ms. Taylor holds an MBA in finance and marketing from the University of Chicago's Booth Graduate School of Business and a BA in economics from the University of Illinois.

Ms. Taylor is married and currently resides with her husband and two daughters in Columbine Valley, Colorado.

CPSIA information can be obtained at www.ICGtesting.com
Printed in the USA
LVOW12s0341070315

429477LV00001B/136/P